W9-CFV-454

Read all of the books in this exciting, action-packed biography series!

Sports Heroes and *LEGENDS*™

TOMBRADY

by Matt Doeden

TFCB Twenty-First Century Books/Minneapolis

Twenty-First Century Books
A division of Lerner Publishing Group, Inc.
241 First Avenue North
Minneapolis, MN 55401 U.S.A.

Website address: www.lernerbooks.com

Cover photograph:
Front cover: © Rob Tringali/SportsChrome
Back cover: © iStockphoto.com/John Mansfield

Library of Congress Cataloging-in-Publication Data

Doeden, Matt.
    Tom Brady / by Matt Doeden.
        p. cm. — (Sports heroes and legends)
    Includes bibliographical references and index.
    ISBN 978-0-7613-4226-7 (lib. bdg. : alk. paper)
    1. Brady, Tom, 1977—Juvenile literature. 2. Football players—United States—
Biography—Juvenile literature. I. Title.
    GV939.B685D64 2009
    796.332092—dc22 [B]   2009004624

Manufactured in the United States of America
1 2 3 4 5 6 – JR – 14 13 12 11 10 09

Contents

Prologue

From Unknown to Champion

One of the most unlikely Super Bowl stories in National Football League (NFL) history emerged in 2001. Twenty-four-year-old Tom Brady had entered training camp as the third-string quarterback of the New England Patriots. He'd barely played in the 2000 season, his first in the NFL, and few experts had expected to see him on the field at all in 2001. But Tom was determined. By the beginning of the season, he'd worked his way up to the backup role. And then he'd filled in at quarterback when longtime starter Drew Bledsoe was injured late in the team's second game.

The Patriots flourished under Tom's leadership and finished 11–5, winning their division. He helped them to a thrilling playoff win over the Oakland Raiders before suffering an ankle injury in a victory over the Pittsburgh Steelers. But he was back on the field for the Super Bowl on February 3, 2002.

New England's opponent was the powerful St. Louis Rams, led by a pass-happy, high-scoring offense nicknamed "the Greatest Show on Turf." Few experts gave New England much hope of winning the game, but the Patriots believed in themselves. They may not have had the raw talent of the Rams, but they played as a single, cohesive unit. They believed the team approach was their biggest advantage. They showed off that mind-set by refusing to go through the traditional individual introductions before the game. Instead, they insisted that they be introduced together as a team, which set the tone for the whole game.

St. Louis opened the scoring with a field goal, but then New England took over. The Patriots' defense frustrated the powerful Rams' offense with a rough, physical style of play. Defensive back Ty Law picked off a pass from St. Louis quarterback Kurt Warner and ran it back for a touchdown. The Rams turned over the ball again with less than 2 minutes remaining in the half. Tom and the offense capitalized. Tom led a quick, efficient drive that ended with an 8-yard touchdown pass to David Patten in the corner of the end zone. Just like that, the Pats were ahead 14–3.

New England extended the lead to 17–3 in the third quarter. But the Rams came storming back in the fourth. Warner scored a rushing touchdown to pull to 17–10. Then, with less than 2 minutes to go, he threw a long touchdown pass to receiver Ricky Proehl, tying the game.

Coach Bill Belichick had a big decision to make. Should he go for the win, or play it safe and go to overtime? He decided to trust his inexperienced quarterback and told Tom to "go win the game."

Tom had a minute and a half to move his team from the 17-yard line into position for a game-winning field-goal attempt. In the huddle, he told his teammates the time had come to end it. "[Tom] said, 'Here we go,'" Patten later told reporters. "He said we have to go down and win the game here. He has just such a tremendous amount of confidence and it revs us up. If you look in his eyes and hear him talk, you think, 'We have to go out and get it done for this kid.'"

Tom was almost flawless on the drive. He moved the ball with short, precise passes. The big play of the drive came when he hooked up with receiver Troy Brown for a 26-yard pass that moved the Patriots to the Rams' 36-yard line. Tom knew that kicker Adam Vinatieri needed to be just a little closer to try a field goal, so he completed one more pass, for 6 yards, to tight end Jermaine Wiggins. That was close enough.

Belichick sent Vinatieri and the field-goal team onto the field with just a few seconds to play. The 48-yard attempt was long, but within Vinatieri's range. The long snapper snapped the ball and Vinatieri calmly booted it through the uprights as the clock struck 0:00.

He'd done it! The Patriots stormed the field in celebration of their 20–17 victory, one of the biggest upsets in Super Bowl history.

Tom, who had completed 16 of 27 pass attempts in the game for 145 yards, was named the Super Bowl Most Valuable Player (MVP). But he gave all of the credit to his team. "This is the perfect example of what happens when guys believe in each other," he told reporters.

Tom Brady had started the season as an unknown. He ended it on top of the football world. The storybook season marked the beginning of a remarkable NFL career.

Chapter One

Two-Sport Star

Thomas Edward Patrick Brady has been a football fan as far back as he can remember. He was born on August 3, 1977, the youngest of Thomas and Galynn Brady's four children. He and his three older sisters—Maureen, Julie, and Nancy—grew up in San Mateo, California, near San Francisco. Tom grew up rooting for the San Francisco 49ers and star quarterback Joe Montana. He and his family spent many a Sunday afternoon at nearby Candlestick Park cheering on Montana and the 49ers.

The only two men among four women, little Tom and his dad formed a tight bond. By the time he was five years old, Tom was playing golf with his dad. "That was kind of their way to get out of the house," said Nancy.

Whatever the game or sport, Tom loved to compete. Whether it was a game of dice with his dad, a video game by himself, or playing sports with his friends, Tom didn't like to lose. Tom's parents both enjoyed sports, and their competitive nature seemed to rub off on all of their children. Tom's sisters all played sports, and Maureen eventually earned a softball scholarship to Fresno State University.

Tom wasn't a fast runner, but he loved to race. He'd challenge faster boys to footraces. If he lost, he'd come back and challenge them again until he won.

"We doted on [Tom], but that only lasted so long," said Julie. "We used to compete for absolutely everything, and we pushed him all the time."

Tom's parents were devout Catholics, and Tom attended Catholic grade school and high school. No matter the sport, he was always one of the better players. He especially excelled in baseball as a catcher. His high school, Junipero Serra High, was known for its great baseball program, but it was not a strong football school. The baseball team had produced future baseball stars, including Jim Fregosi and Barry Bonds.

Sure enough, Tom did well on Serra's baseball team. But he was also determined to be on the football team, perhaps dreaming of doing his best impression of his idol, Joe Montana, on the field. He started out on defense, as a linebacker. After his freshman year, he finally got his chance to play quarterback for the junior varsity team. Tom worked hard to make the most of the opportunity. He studied the position and worked with a personal coach on his approach and form. When someone told him that he had a great arm but lacked the agility and speed to be a Division I college quarterback, he put himself through drill after drill to improve his footwork.

JOE MONTANA

One of Tom's football heroes is quarterback Joe Montana. Their careers have been similar in many ways. Montana struggled to get playing time during his college days at Notre Dame. He was a later draft pick, going to the 49ers in the third round of the 1979 draft. But Montana exceeded all expectations, winning four Super Bowls and throwing for 273 touchdown passes over his fifteen-year career. The two-time MVP and Hall of Famer is one of the NFL's all-time great passers.

"I've never been real fleet of foot," he later said. "I enjoyed the struggle of [improving]. I gained a lot out of it, in terms of mental toughness."

By his sophomore year, Tom was playing for the Junipero Serra High Padres varsity team as a backup. As a junior, he took over the role of full-time starter. But sometimes Tom's hard work didn't seem to be paying off. The Padres still weren't much of a football team, losing about as many games as they won. In his junior season, Tom put up great individual numbers, but they didn't translate into team success. At one point, Serra lost two straight games by a combined total of 110–6.

After the mediocre season, Coach Tom MacKenzie called Tom into his office. MacKenzie explained to Tom that the coaches weren't nominating him for All-League honors, despite the fact that the young quarterback had posted solid numbers.

"We knew he was capable of doing better," MacKenzie later explained. "And we wanted to get across the message that things in life are earned, not given."

Due in part to success in some summer football camps, college scouts were interested in Tom as he entered his senior season in 1994. But unfortunately, the team, finishing just 5–5, did little to boost the 17-year-old's stock. Over his two seasons as the varsity quarterback, Tom completed 219 passes for 3,514 yards. They were very good numbers, but the lack of team success could hurt Tom. He had performed poorly in the team's final two games, when he could have helped them earn a play-off berth.

For college scouts, Tom had a mixed résumé. His arm was good, but his feet were slow. His teams had failed to win, and he'd been unable to come through in the clutch. Would his statistics alone be enough to impress the nation's top college football programs?

❝[Tom is] confident, but not arrogant. He believes in himself, but it's not cockiness.❞

—Junipero Serra High football coach Tom MacKenzie

Baseball, however, was another matter. Tom had continued to star for Serra's baseball team, and major league scouts took notice. In the spring of 1995, after Tom's senior season, the Montreal Expos (later known as the Washington Nationals) drafted Tom in the eighteenth round of the major league amateur draft. According to one scout, he would have gone much higher in the draft if he hadn't been so determined to play football instead.

"[Tom was] a definite prospect," said Florida Marlins scout Gary Hughes. "[He was] a big catcher, and sometimes you shy away from big catchers, but he was projected as a power hitter with a very good arm who handled pitchers well."

Despite a generous contract offer from the Expos, Tom's mind was made up. He wanted to play football. So he and his parents made a video of his highlights at Serra and sent it to fifty-five major college coaches. The tactic worked. Coaches noticed his raw athleticism. And once one major school showed interest, others followed. Soon, coaches from major football universities such as the University of Southern California (USC), the University of California (Cal), and the University of Illinois were after Tom. Later, Michigan entered the Tom Brady sweepstakes. Despite heavy recruitment from USC, Tom decided to leave California and head to Michigan.

"He was our number one guy, the key to our whole recruiting class," said Cal coach Keith Gilbertson. "[Losing Tom to Michigan] was a real blow to us, quite a loss."

Tom could have stayed in California, where he would be close to home and assured of playing time. But that wasn't what he was all about. The inscription under his picture in his high school yearbook explained it all: "If you want to play with the big boys, you've got to learn to play in the tall grass." And so he was off to Michigan.

Chapter Two

Wolverine

T he University of Michigan had one of the top college football programs in the nation. Its team name was the Wolverines, and they drew more than 100,000 fans to every home game. The team was a virtual NFL factory, turning out dozens and dozens of professional stars. The Wolverines played in the tough Big Ten conference, meaning that Tom and his teammates would be facing some of the stiffest competition in the nation.

But all was not well. Tom had decided on Michigan largely because of two of its coaches—head coach Gary Moeller and an assistant named Tommy Harris. But the summer of 1995 brought change to the Michigan staff. Moeller was fired after an off-the-field incident, and Harris left for another job. Tom didn't know a lot about the new coach, Lloyd Carr. And worse, Carr didn't know a lot about Tom. The situation concerned Tom, and he often talked about it with his dad. Although

Tom was on his own, he still frequently sought advice from his father.

MICHIGAN TRADITION

The University of Michigan, in Ann Arbor, Michigan, has one of the most successful college football programs in history. The school won its first national championship in 1901, the first of four in a row. The school has won a total of eleven national titles, along with forty-two Big Ten titles.

"My first recollection of Tom was during a scrimmage in fall practice, and he was with the third team," Carr later said. "He kept . . . throwing the ball right on the money. I don't know what he weighed back then—185 [pounds] maybe. But he got beat up pretty good that day, and you could tell he was really competitive and real tough."

Tom may have made a good first impression, but Carr still redshirted him in his first year. A redshirted player can practice with the team but cannot dress for or play in any games. This time is a chance for a player to get a taste of college football without losing one of his four years of college eligibility. Carr's decision also gave Tom a chance to focus more on his classes. He'd always been a good student in high school, and he took his studies seriously. So Tom watched as Carr and the Wolverines finished the season 9–4 (5–3 in the Big Ten) and then lost to Texas A&M in the Alamo Bowl, 22–20.

Because he'd been redshirted, Tom's second year in college—1996—was considered his freshman year in terms of football. He could finally dress for games. But that didn't mean Carr had much playing time for him. Once again, Tom spent most of his time watching and cheering on his teammates. The Wolverines were stocked at the quarterback position: Brian Griese and Scott Driesbach were the top two quarterbacks. That made Tom the third-string passer. He played in only two games that year, both times in a mop-up role (meaning the outcome of the games was already decided). His first pass was a disaster. Against UCLA, he dropped back and tried to fire the ball to a receiver. But a linebacker stepped up and intercepted the ball, returning it for a touchdown. Not a good start! Tom attempted only five passes all season. He completed three of them for a total of 26 yards.

Finally, in 1997, Tom got a chance to compete for playing time. He was prepared to battle Griese for the starting job. During training camp, Tom felt like he had proved himself and earned the job. But Carr disagreed and named Griese the starter. Tom would be his backup. The news was devastating to Tom. He was starting his third year at Michigan and was barely playing. For a time, he thought about quitting. In the end, Tom decided that he'd just work harder. Even as a backup, he could get some playing time and so he needed to stay ready. The support of his family was a big help. Tom's parents often traveled to games, even though they knew there was little chance they'd actually see Tom play.

66*Coach Carr was truly doing what he thought was best for the team and he was right in his perspective. Sometimes I disagreed with it, but I would never change a day in my life, especially the lessons I learned there because those have really suited me well on the professional level.*99

—TOM ON HIS STRUGGLES TO GET PLAYING TIME AT MICHIGAN

Carr's decision to go with Griese ultimately proved to be a wise move. Griese played very well and led the Wolverines to a perfect 11–0 regular-season record. Tom, as the backup, played in four games, completing 12 of 15 passes for 103 yards. The Wolverines faced off against the Washington Huskies in the Rose Bowl in January 1998. Tom watched from the sidelines as Griese led Michigan to a 21–16 win and a share of the national championship.

Late in the 1997 season, Tom was rushed to the hospital with appendicitis. While in the hospital, he lost 30 pounds and much of his strength. He didn't play again that year.

After the season, Tom again wondered if his decision to attend Michigan had been a mistake. He liked the school and was doing well in his classes. He was working toward a degree in business and took his education very seriously. According to one teammate, Tom would get very angry if he ever received a grade that was lower than he had expected. Tom was also involved in the community and volunteered at a local children's hospital with several of his teammates. He was popular among his classmates and teammates, and he enjoyed an active social life on campus. But from a football standpoint, he wasn't getting a chance. Had the time come to cut his losses and transfer to Cal? He knew he'd get playing time there. He discussed it with his dad and Carr. In the end, Tom decided to stay with the Wolverines.

Carr told reporters that Tom was the leading candidate to be the quarterback in 1998. "Tom Brady, who made significant progress in the fall, will go in as the number one quarterback,"

Carr said. But then he added, "If he throws the ball to the other team, the bench is waiting for him." It was hardly a vote of confidence.

TRAPPED

Before his junior season, Tom drove to Notre Dame Stadium to get a look at the place. He knew that Michigan would be playing there that season. He walked into the stadium, finding an unlocked gate. But then he couldn't get back out. He tried gate after gate and found himself locked in. He finally found a ladder, which he used to climb over a wall to make his escape.

Tom trained hard that summer. He was determined to be the starter and to succeed. His success was far from a sure thing, however. Griese had moved on to the NFL, but Michigan had added a freshman quarterback. Drew Henson, from nearby Brighton, Michigan, was already something of a legend in the region. He'd been heavily recruited as a quarterback. And baseball's New York Yankees had drafted him and signed him to a huge contract of $4.5 million. The contract would take effect as soon as Henson was ready to leave college. Henson was a tremendous natural athlete and considered one of the brightest prospects in the nation. Carr was under heavy pressure to make the local phenom the starter. Rumors swirled that Carr had promised Henson the starting job, just to get him to come to Michigan. Tom must have been wondering about his place on the team when, before the season, Carr described Henson as the most talented quarterback he'd ever coached.

Still, Carr went with Tom as his starter for the opener at Notre Dame. The Wolverines dominated the Fighting Irish in the first half but failed to capitalize on the scoreboard. They took a 13–6 lead into halftime. In the second half, Notre Dame dominated every phase of the game, handing Michigan a 36–20 defeat. In his first college start, Tom went 23–36 (23 completions in 36 pass attempts) for 216 yards.

"I thought he played well," Carr said. "I thought he showed a lot of maturity for playing as well as he did in an environment such as Notre Dame Stadium."

Regardless, many Wolverine fans were calling for Henson. Brady remained largely an unknown, and the fans wanted to see the local star.

Things only got worse for Tom the next week against Syracuse. He threw an early interception, and Carr decided to give Henson a shot. The packed house at Michigan cheered loudly as Henson took the field. Then later, Carr put Tom back in. And then Henson again. In the end, the musical chairs at quarterback didn't seem to matter. Syracuse was clearly the better team and won the game 38–28. The Michigan fans, unused to their team starting a season 0–2, turned on Brady. They wanted Henson, and they wanted him *now*.

Tom rallied his teammates. He called them together to talk about the bad start to the season. He was the quarterback and a team leader, and he was acting the part. That was a big reason why many of his teammates favored him over Henson.

Carr continued to give Henson some playing time, but Brady remained his primary quarterback. Tom rewarded his coach. He earned his first win as a starter the next week against Eastern Michigan. Tom got most of the playing time, completing 14 of 19 passes for 128 yards in a 59–20 victory. Next, Tom and the Wolverines opened their Big Ten schedule with a 29–17 victory over Michigan State. The big play in the game came in the second quarter with the score tied 10–10. Tom took the snap and dropped back. He spotted receiver Tai Streets running toward the back of the end zone. Tom lofted a high pass to the corner of the end zone, and Streets reached over a defender to haul it in. The touchdown gave Michigan a lead that they wouldn't relinquish. "I made the play and I'm just happy [Tom] gave me a chance," Streets said of his big catch.

Michigan kept rolling with wins over Iowa, Northwestern, Indiana, and Minnesota. On November 7, the Wolverines hosted a powerful 6–1 Penn State team. Penn State was ranked ninth in the nation and was looking to take control of the Big Ten. But Tom and his teammates were ready.

The Wolverines' defense smothered Penn State early on, while Tom led the offense. He found fullback Aaron Shea on the sideline for a 26-yard touchdown pass to give the Wolverines the lead. Later in the first quarter, Tom hit Streets with a touchdown pass in the corner of the end zone. Michigan just kept pounding, running up a shocking 27–0 victory. It was their seventh win in a row, and they were in first place in the Big Ten with a conference mark of 6–0.

"That was real nice," Tom said after the win. "I think you saw a Michigan team really fired up. This was the most enthusiastic we've been in eight weeks."

A win over Wisconsin the next week was Michigan's eighth in a row. "Anytime you win a few in a row, you start to feel good about yourself," Tom told the school newspaper. "Fortunately, we've been able to keep winning, and now we've got one more to go."

That one game was a showdown with the Ohio State Buckeyes, ranked number seven in the nation. The two teams were playing for a share of the Big Ten title and possibly a trip to the Rose Bowl (the winner of the Big Ten traditionally plays in the Rose Bowl).

Buckeye coach John Cooper praised Tom before the game. "Brady does a good job," Cooper said. "He's not flashy. He's not spectacular, but he does what the coaches ask him to do. He stays within the game plan and doesn't beat himself."

In the end, the Wolverines were no match for the Buckeyes. The Ohio State offense rolled over the Michigan defense, and Tom and his offense couldn't keep up. The 31–16 loss ended Michigan's winning streak. They were left with a bid to the Citrus Bowl instead of the Rose Bowl, where they would face the Arkansas Razorbacks.

The Arkansas defense was a quick, aggressive unit. Many fans suggested that Henson was much better suited to playing against that style. Brady was a pure pocket passer who had trouble evading the pass rush (the pocket is the area immediately behind the offensive line). Henson, meanwhile, was an all-around great athlete with the ability to escape defenders.

Tom started the game and led Michigan to a field goal on their opening drive. Then Carr switched to Henson for a series (offensive possession). When Henson's series went nowhere, Tom was back in for the rest of the game. Michigan held a 24–10 halftime lead, but Arkansas stormed back in the third quarter with 21 straight points. Tom was playing poorly, having thrown two interceptions that led to Arkansas scores.

Trailing by 7 points, Tom's approach changed—for the better. "I don't exactly know why [being behind] loosens you up," Tom said. "Sometimes you're out there and you're playing and you don't want to make a mistake. But once you make a mistake, you go, 'Golly, I'm not too successful thinking that way.'"

Tom promptly led two straight scoring drives. On the first, he took the Wolverines 80 yards down the field. He completed a big 15-yard pass on a third-and-11 play (third down, 11 yards to get a first down) and then an 8-yarder on a critical fourth-and-2. Running back Anthony Thomas capped the drive with the tying touchdown. Tom and the offense went right back to work when they got back the ball. Tom's 21-yard touchdown pass to DiAllo Johnson gave Michigan the lead, and they never looked back. The Wolverines won the game 45–31 and finished the season ranked twelfth in the nation. They hadn't won a national championship, but their finish was strong after the rough 0–2 start. Michigan fans had plenty of reasons to look forward to the 1999 season.

Chapter Three

Making the Jump

After a rough start, Tom had pieced together a brilliant junior season. He had the confidence of his teammates, who voted him a team captain. But the quarterback controversy just wouldn't go away. Shockingly, Carr announced a plan to use both quarterbacks during the 1999 season. Tom would start each game, but Henson would take over in the second quarter. Then the coaches would decide which quarterback to use in the second half. Many experts scoffed at the decision. They said it was Carr trying to find any way to keep Henson from leaving school to play baseball.

"I'm not saying [Tom] did or didn't like it," said Michigan offensive coordinator Mike DeBord. "Yet Tom Brady never flinched, never complained. He took a difficult situation and handled it beautifully."

Many saw Carr's decision as a slap in the face to Tom. Tom had the support of his teammates and could easily have raised a fuss. But he didn't do that. Tom didn't like the decision, but he made the best of it. He never let the situation affect his dedication or preparation. According to a Michigan athletic counselor, Tom relied on his religious faith (he was raised as a devout Catholic) to help get him through the difficult situation.

❝I don't think either [Tom or Henson] was happy with it. I expected they would handle it in a way that wouldn't divide the team, but Tom, as a captain and as a fifth-year senior, I know it had to be tougher on him. I wouldn't have done it that way if I didn't know what kind of person he was.❞

—LLOYD CARR ON HIS DECISION TO SPLIT TIME
BETWEEN TOM AND DREW HENSON IN 1999

The quarterback experiment started with the opener against Notre Dame. After Tom and Henson each had a turn, the Wolverines found themselves trailing 14–9 at halftime. In the locker room, Carr made his decision—Tom was his man. The 22-year-old quarterback led his offense to 10 straight points and a 19–14 lead. But with about 4 minutes to play in the game, Notre Dame scored to take a 22–19 lead. Tom led his offense onto the field knowing that he needed a field goal to tie or a touchdown to win.

If he was nervous, he didn't let his teammates know. In the huddle, he said, "What an opportunity." Then he went out and seized that opportunity. From the Notre Dame 25-yard line, he dropped back and scanned the field. He saw receiver David Terrell open and fired a perfect 20-yard pass down the field. A few plays later, running back Anthony Thomas punched in the game-winning touchdown—26–22 Michigan. In the game, Tom had completed 17 of 24 passes for 197 yards (Henson, meanwhile, had gone just 3 of 8 for 40 yards).

"You beat Notre Dame . . . it doesn't get much better than that," Tom said after the game. "You prepare for situations like this in the summer and with conditioning, and you think you'll pounce on them. But every time you play Notre Dame, they have the type of players and the tradition to make it a dogfight."

The victory was the beginning of a winning streak for Michigan. The team went on to win its first five games. In each game, Henson played the second quarter, but Tom was always back in for the second half. The only bad news in the streak was that in a win over Wisconsin, Tom suffered a concussion (bruise to the brain) that forced him to the sidelines for the rest of the game.

The five-game winning streak was capped with a 38–12 drubbing of Purdue, which had been undefeated coming into the contest. The game had been built up as a big showdown between two powerful offenses. Purdue's Drew Brees was one of the best passers in college football and considered by many to be a future NFL quarterback. But Purdue was no match for Michigan. Tom was back on the field, and the Wolverines jumped out to a 14–3 lead after one quarter. They never looked back.

Tom completed 15 of 25 passes for 250 yards in the win. But after the game, he wasn't interested in talking about individual stats. "I'm just happy about being 5-0," he told reporters.

Things were going well. Tom was clearly the more prepared quarterback, and the team was winning under his leadership. But for some reason, Carr decided to change the formula for the sixth game of the season. The Wolverines were facing the Michigan State Spartans. Carr decided that each quarterback would play half of the game. Tom would get the first and fourth quarters, while Henson would play the second and third. The decision mystified many. Why would Carr mess with a system that was working?

The first half went as planned. But Henson struggled badly in the third quarter, and Tom was ready when Carr sent him back into the game. But with the Wolverines already trailing 27–10, was it too late? Had Carr waited too long to go back to his senior quarterback?

Tom did all he could. He led Michigan up and down the field, frantically trying to stage a comeback. The teams traded touchdowns. Down 17 points, Tom found Terrell open in the corner of the end zone. He lofted a soft touch pass that landed right in the wide receiver's arms.

The Wolverines, down 10, got the ball back on their own 4-yard line. Tom just kept going. He was throwing the ball all over the field, hitting receivers with one pinpoint pass after another. He completed 9 of 11 passes on the drive for 86 yards, including one to Aaron Shea for a touchdown. But in the end, he just didn't have enough time. Michigan State held on for a 34–31 win, dropping the Wolverines to 5–1 on the season and all but ending any national title hopes they might have had.

Tom refused to place the blame for the loss on the strange situation with the quarterback position. "We just didn't put together four quarters of football," he said. "We came on at the end, but to beat a team like this, you need to play 60 minutes."

The next week brought another loss, this time 35–29 to Illinois. Henson did little in limited playing time, while Tom completed 22 of 28 passes for 307 yards and two touchdowns. With that, Carr's quarterback experiment was over. Tom Brady was the full-time quarterback for the Wolverines.

The team rallied around him. They used a late field goal to beat Indiana 34–31. Then they blew out Northwestern 37–3, a win that vaulted them to the number-16 ranking in the nation. The remaining schedule was brutal, however, with games on the road against powerful sixth-ranked Penn State and at home against archrival Ohio State.

The Wolverines surprised Penn State by building a 10-point lead early, but the Nittany Lions fought back. Midway through the fourth quarter, Tom and his teammates trailed 27–17. But they shocked the Penn State crowd by scoring two touchdowns in less than two minutes to earn an upset victory. The comeback started with an 81-yard drive that Tom finished off with a touchdown run. Michigan's defense stopped Penn State on the next possession, and Tom came onto the field needing a field goal to tie or a touchdown to win. Tom hit Marcus Knight with two big passes on the drive, including the winning touchdown.

"We're just battling and battling until that clock says 0:00," Tom said. "It might not always be pretty. You're going to make a lot of mistakes. You just got to find a way to win."

66_You want to be decisive. You want to make good throws. If you're tentative, you're not successful. I've learned that the hard way._**99**

—TOM'S PHILOSOPHY
DURING HIS SENIOR SEASON AT MICHIGAN

Tom led Michigan to another comeback win in the final game of the regular season. His fourth-quarter touchdown pass to Marquise Walker gave the Wolverines a 24–17 win and an overall record of 9–2 (6–2 in the Big Ten) and moved them to the number-eight ranking in the nation. That was good enough to earn them an invitation to the Orange Bowl, where they would square off against the sixth-ranked Alabama Crimson Tide. It would be Tom's last college game.

Alabama's coaches believed that Michigan's strength was its running game. So they packed Alabama's defenders close to the line of scrimmage, signaling to the Wolverines that if they were going to move the ball, it had to be through the air. The strategy was a direct challenge to Tom's abilities.

Early on, the strategy worked. Carr was determined to run the ball, despite the Alabama defense. The Wolverines did little through the air in the first half, with the exception of a long touchdown pass from Tom to Terrell. In the second half, however, the Michigan offense got back on track. Carr realized that just running the ball wasn't going to be enough. He needed to rely on Tom's arm. Tom responded by spreading the ball all over the field, hitting receivers on pass after pass.

The third quarter was an intense back-and-forth battle, with the teams combining for a total of 35 points. Tom and his offense erased a 14-point deficit and, late in the fourth quarter, had a chance to win the game. But Alabama blocked a Michigan field-goal attempt, sending the game into overtime.

In college football's overtime, each team gets the ball at the opponent's 25-yard line. They get one drive to score. If either team leads at the end of the period, the game is over. If they're still tied, they play another overtime period. After a coin toss, Tom and the Wolverines got the ball first. Tom didn't waste any time. On the first play, he dropped back and spotted tight end Shawn Thompson streaking down the middle of the field. He rifled a pass that Thompson hauled in for a touchdown. With the extra point, the Wolverines led 35–28. Alabama needed a touchdown and an extra point to force another overtime. They took only two plays to get the touchdown, but shockingly, they missed the extra point. The game was over—Michigan had won the Orange Bowl 35–34!

In the game, Tom had completed 31 of 46 passes for 369 yards and four touchdowns—all Orange Bowl records. He had given every bit of energy he could. After the game, he could barely walk off the field. His dad had to carry his equipment bag for him.

Tom had put up great numbers during his senior season. He'd completed 214 of 341 passes for 2,586 yards and twenty touchdowns. He'd thrown only six interceptions. He'd proved himself against the highest level of college competition. Yet questions about his future in the NFL remained. He had a great arm and was a natural leader, but some NFL teams questioned his foot speed. Others wondered why he hadn't been the full-time starter at Michigan for the whole year. Mel Kiper Jr., an analyst who many consider an NFL draft expert, dismissed Tom's potential, saying he "didn't have the total package of skills."

To make things worse, Tom didn't perform well at the Senior Bowl, an all-star game in which players coming out of college show off their stuff for scouts. And his performance at the NFL Combine (a series of tests put on by NFL teams) had been a dud. He'd run the 40-yard dash in an embarrassingly slow 5.23 seconds and had scored just 24.5 inches on his vertical leap (although he had scored very well on the tests that measured organization and leadership skills). His draft stock plummeted.

Still, some teams, including the New England Patriots, showed interest. Dick Rehbein, the Patriots' quarterbacks coach, had seen Tom play. He thought the 22-year-old had potential. Could he convince head coach Bill Belichick?

On April 20, 2000, Tom and his family gathered in their living room to watch the draft on television. The first round came and went. So did the second round. It was a long, difficult day of watching pick after pick. Tom couldn't stand the waiting, so he went to a baseball game in the afternoon.

The draft continued the next day. These later rounds were when Tom really expected to be picked. But the names kept coming, and Tom kept waiting. As the Patriots' pick in the fifth round approached, Tom was hopeful. But New England didn't take him.

"He was so angry and hurt," said his sister Nancy. "With what happened at Michigan, and now having this infuriating and disappointing couple of days, he just wanted to take a walk, and he grabbed a bat."

Tom used that bat to take out some of his frustration in the backyard. But before long, the phone finally rang. It was Belichick, asking for Tom. Tom's dad told the coach that Tom was in the shower, not wanting to reveal that he was really out back having a temper tantrum. They quickly called Tom inside, and Belichick told him that New England had made him their sixth-round draft choice, the 199th overall pick in the draft.

❝It was the way Michigan handled him. There wasn't a whole lot to go on. He was splitting time with a freshman. . . . If he's not starting in college, what's going to make you think he's going to come in and save your franchise?**❞**

—BILL BELICHICK ON WHY SO MANY TEAMS PASSED ON TOM IN THE DRAFT

Tom was determined to prove that the Pats had made a good choice. He quickly signed a contract for $298,000 per year

31

and started learning the playbook. The Patriots had four quarterbacks on the roster, and Tom would be last in the pecking order. He knew that his rookie year would be a lot like his redshirt year at Michigan. But he had a chance to learn the game and get some practice. He wasn't likely to see any real time on the playing field. In fact, there was no guarantee that he'd even make the team.

 In the spring of 2000, Tom graduated from Michigan with a business degree in organizational studies.

Tom did make the team. He memorized the playbook long before training camp and worked as hard as he could. He was on the roster, but his main role was to practice with the team's other young players.

"He kind of took them over," said offensive coordinator Charlie Weis of Tom's role with the group of young players. "And you just watched the whole group mature around him. It wasn't that they all could play. You just watched them all mature because he would always strive to be the best, because he'd work harder than anyone else in the weight room."

Tom was making the best of his situation. Few thought he'd be the Pats' quarterback anytime soon. Starter Drew Bledsoe had just signed a ten-year contract extension worth $103 million. So Tom watched from the sidelines—more often than not, he wasn't even listed on the active roster. He played in only one game—a 34–7 blowout loss to the Detroit Lions on Thanksgiving Day. Tom threw three passes in the game, completing just one for 6 yards. Another of his passes was almost intercepted.

"You've got to prepare each week like you're going to [start], and if you do that, you know you're ready," Tom said. "That's the approach I've taken the whole season. I always prepare like I'm going to be in there, and the coach tells me whether I'm dressing this week. There were times I didn't dress, but at least I was prepared. You never know what's going to happen."

Aside from that brief time on the field, Tom just watched and observed. What he saw wasn't always pretty. The Patriots struggled to a 5–11 finish. They weren't very good, and many fans were calling for Belichick to be fired. The picture for the Patriots looked dismal. What would the 2001 season hold for Tom and the Patriots?

Chapter Four

Out of the Blue

Tom's rookie season had been a great learning experience. But for 2001, he wasn't going to be content just to stand on the sidelines. He told Weis that he expected to compete for more than just the backup role—an ambitious goal considering that Bledsoe was the face of the New England Patriots.

In fact, during the off-season, Belichick and the Pats' coaching staff didn't even view Tom as the number-two man. They signed Damon Huard to a contract worth more than $1 million to serve as Bledsoe's backup.

After his years at Michigan, Tom knew all about fighting to climb up the depth chart. So he worked hard even before training camp began. In camp, his hard work and accurate throwing made the coaching staff take notice. Soon, Tom wasn't just number three—he was competing with Huard for the backup role.

On August 6, tragedy struck. Dick Rehbein, New England's quarterbacks coach and the man who had convinced Belichick to draft Tom, died suddenly of a heart attack. The loss was a terrible shock for Tom and his teammates. Tom kept working hard, though. Rehbein had shown faith in him, and Tom was going to prove that the coach's faith had been well placed. Tom had a fantastic training camp, playing well in practice as well as the preseason games. Soon, Belichick surprised everyone by announcing that Tom, not Huard, would be Bledsoe's primary backup. Belichick said that both quarterbacks had played well but that Tom had just done more to earn the spot.

"It was a big decision, but it wasn't a hard decision," the coach said. "The only thing that happened was that Brady played better in the preseason, so he got more snaps in practice because we felt like we needed to see him play."

The season began with a 23–17 loss to the Cincinnati Bengals. Two days later, on September 11, terrorists attacked the United States, flying airplanes into the World Trade Center in New York and the Pentagon in Washington, D.C. The NFL postponed the next week's games as the nation struggled to deal with the crisis.

The Patriots were back on the field on September 23 for their home opener against the New York Jets. The game was a disaster for Bledsoe and the New England offense. Bledsoe made several critical mistakes and the offense was stagnant. In the fourth quarter, Bledsoe tried to make a play with his legs, running the ball down the sideline. Jets' linebacker Mo Lewis slammed into him with a violent tackle. Bledsoe was down and hurt. He tried to stay in the game, but eventually Tom had to come in.

The Patriots were trailing 10–3 when Tom entered the game. He didn't have much time. He went to work on the New York defense, completing several short, safe passes. The team was moving down the field. But time was running out. Tom had to throw a couple of Hail Mary (long, desperate) passes to tie the game. But the passes fell incomplete, and the Patriots lost the game. In his limited time, Tom had completed 5 of 10 passes for 46 yards.

"I thought [Tom] did OK with what he had there," Belichick said. "All things considered, I thought in that situation he threw the ball pretty accurately and made good decisions."

Belichick would need Tom to continue making those good decisions. Bledsoe had damaged a blood vessel in his chest and would miss several games. The situation looked bleak for New England. They were 0–2 and had to start an untested second-year quarterback. To many, the team's playoff hopes seemed all but dead.

Tom and his teammates didn't see the situation that way. Tom made his first start as an NFL quarterback September 30 against the Indianapolis Colts, led by a young star quarterback named Peyton Manning. Manning and the Colts had one of the best offenses in football, but the day belonged to Tom and the Patriots. Tom's job was simple: take care of the ball and don't make mistakes. That's exactly what he did. He completed just 13 of 23 passes for 168 yards, but that performance was more than enough. The Patriot defense returned two Manning interceptions for touchdowns and cruised to an easy 44–13 victory. His performance left many fans wondering just how he'd accomplished the win.

"I've always had high expectations for myself," Tom explained. "I set my goals high. I've been prepared for this. It's not as if they pulled me off the street and said, 'You're starting.'"

Tom struggled in his second game as a starter, against the Miami Dolphins. The Pats' record dropped to 1–3. The team needed to turn things around and fast.

The season turned around for New England on October 14, when they hosted the San Diego Chargers. In Tom's third NFL start, he finally threw his first touchdown pass, a 21-yarder to receiver Terry Glenn in the first half. But still, the Chargers seemed to be firmly in control of the game, leading late in the fourth quarter.

New England had to throw the ball because running it would eat up too much clock. Tom put the ball in the air on play after play. The passing attack was controlled and precise, and Tom led the Patriots to two straight scoring drives. With a field goal and a touchdown, New England tied the game and forced a sudden-death overtime. San Diego started with the ball, but the Patriot defense stopped them, giving Tom and his offense a chance.

On New England's first offensive play, Tom stepped to the line and surveyed the defense. He noticed that the Chargers were lined up in a formation he'd seen before. They looked like they were setting up for a blitz (a play in which the defense sends extra men to rush the quarterback). Tom quickly barked out signals to his teammates. He was calling an audible (changing the play). In the new play, receiver David Patten would make a quick move down the sideline, while the offensive line and running back would work to stop the heavy pass rush. The key was for Tom to get rid of the ball quickly, and the play worked perfectly. As expected, the blitz came, and Tom lofted a pass toward Patten along the sideline. The San Diego defender interfered with Patten, drawing a key penalty that moved the ball down the field.

Tom's teammates were impressed with his poise. "I've been saying it all along," said veteran center Damien Woody. "[Tom] doesn't play like an inexperienced quarterback. He saw that there was a situation and he put us in position to take advantage of it."

The play helped put kicker Adam Vinatieri into field-goal range. He booted a 44-yarder to win the game, 29–26. The comeback was complete. The legend of Tom Brady was just beginning. "That was the game when everything changed," Weis later said.

Tom was named NFL Player of the Week for his comeback performance against San Diego. In the game, he completed 33 of 54 passes for 364 yards and two touchdowns.

Next up was a rematch with the Colts. Tom's confidence was sky-high against a weak Indy defense. Once again, Tom played virtually error-free football, spreading the ball all over the field. His biggest play of the game came on a 91-yard touchdown pass to Patten—the longest passing touchdown in New England history. The Pats won the game in a blowout, 38–17.

Even so, Tom was still inexperienced, and occasionally it showed. In a loss to Denver, for example, he threw four interceptions. But on the whole, the Patriots had improved drastically with Tom at the helm.

By late November, Bledsoe was healthy again. People started to wonder what Belichick would do. An unwritten rule in the NFL was that a player shouldn't lose his job because of an injury. But Tom was winning games. He was making few of the mistakes that had plagued Bledsoe.

Tom didn't throw an interception in his first 162 NFL passes. That was the longest streak to start a career in NFL history.

Belichick stuck with Tom. The decision made national headlines. Many wondered how he could go with Tom—a 24-year-old whom few had even heard of before the season—over Bledsoe, who had recently signed a contract worth more than $100 million.

The decision was tough on everyone—Belichick, Bledsoe, and even Tom. He knew the feeling of losing playing time to another quarterback under controversial circumstances. "There are feelings you fight," he explained. "One of your teammates and friends isn't as happy as he normally is. . . . I don't know if uncomfortable is the word. You want to play and you anticipate playing. Someone else not being in the situation they want to be in, it's definitely a difficult situation." In the end, Tom proved Belichick right. He and the Patriots lost just one more game that season, a 24–17 nail-biter to the St. Louis Rams, a team considered by many to be the best in the league.

66Drew's been more supportive than I could have hoped for. Our relationship has taken on a different role and I completely understand that. We've always been friends. He's been here nine years and he's done a great job.99

—Tom Brady

After the loss to St. Louis, the Pats got hot. They won their last five regular-season games to clinch the American Football Conference (AFC) East division title and earn a playoff spot. Tom continued to play beyond his years, making smart decisions and taking care of the football. His careful approach helped New England to one close victory after another. He didn't always put up big numbers, but he always seemed to do just enough to give his team a chance to win.

With their 11–5 record, the Patriots had earned a first-round bye (week off) in the playoffs. They opened their playoffs in the divisional round, hosting the Oakland Raiders. Snow was falling steadily onto the field at Foxboro Stadium. The scene was set for one of the most memorable—and controversial—games in NFL history.

At first, the game wasn't exactly action packed. Both offenses struggled to move the ball in the snowstorm. Oakland took a 7–0 lead into halftime and stretched that margin to 13–3 after three quarters.

In the fourth quarter, the Patriots used a no-huddle offense to pick up the pace. The strategy worked. Tom spread the ball around the snow-covered field, moving the team deep into Oakland territory. He capped off the drive by running the ball himself into the end zone for a touchdown. The Oakland lead was down to 3 points.

The Patriot defense stopped the Raiders and got the ball back for the offense. Time was quickly running out, however. Tom remained calm and continued to complete passes and move the ball downfield. Still needing at least 10 yards to get into field-goal range, Tom took the snap and dropped back. He cocked the ball back, searching for an open receiver. But nobody was open, so he started to bring the ball back down toward his body.

BOOM! Just as Tom was bringing the ball forward, Oakland's Charles Woodson slammed into him from behind. The ball popped out of Tom's grasp, and an Oakland defender fell onto it. With the fumble recovery, the Raiders would take control of the ball and could eat up the rest of the clock to end the game. The Oakland sideline celebrated what looked like a huge win while the officials reviewed the play on instant replay. When the referee came out to announce the decision, almost everyone was shocked by what he said. He announced that because Tom's arm was moving forward when the ball came out, it was an incomplete pass, not a fumble. New England got to keep the ball. An obscure NFL rule said that the quarterback's intent didn't matter. By the letter of the rule, what Tom did was considered an incomplete pass even though Tom had never meant to throw the ball. Tom took advantage of the lucky break. He hit Patten with a 13-yard pass to set up the game-tying field goal from Vinatieri. Overtime!

New England got the ball first, and Tom went to work. He methodically moved the team down the field with crisp, safe passes. At one point, he completed eight passes in a row. Oakland never fully recovered from the controversial call. Soon, Tom had driven the team into range for a game-winning field-goal attempt.

> ❝*Everybody's talking about [Tom] being a second-year quarterback. Well, he's a student of the game. He's composed. . . . He's a leader. He leads with his excitement and also his calmness and poise in the huddle during tight situations.*❞
> —PATRIOT OFFENSIVE LINEMAN STACY COMPTON
> AFTER NEW ENGLAND'S PLAYOFF WIN OVER THE RAIDERS

After the game, Tom wouldn't quite admit it, but clearly he knew that he'd gotten away with a huge mistake. "Yeah, I was throwing the ball," he said with a guilty grin. "[Woodson] hit me as I was throwing. How do you like that?"

"Watching him, you'd think he had ten years in this league," Vinatieri said of his quarterback. "He just has so much poise. He didn't razzle-dazzle and woo you to death. He just makes plays."

Vinatieri did his part, booting the ball through the uprights to complete an amazing 16–13 victory. The win earned New England a trip to Pittsburgh, where they'd face off with the Steelers in the AFC Championship. The winner would be headed to the Super Bowl.

The Steelers had a rough, hard-hitting defense. Tom found that out the hard way in the second quarter. He dropped back to pass. Pittsburgh safety Lee Flowers, on a blitz, slammed into Tom's lower body. Tom fell to the ground with a badly twisted ankle. He had to come out of the game, and it was Drew Bledsoe to the rescue. The veteran quarterback stepped in and played well, leading New England to several scores and a 24–17 victory. The Patriots were going to the Super Bowl!

 Tom was selected to the Pro Bowl (all-star game) after the 2001 season. On the season, he completed 264 of 413 passes for 2,843 yards and 18 touchdowns.

Everyone wanted to know what Belichick would do. Bledsoe had played well and had experience playing in a Super Bowl. Tom's ankle might not be 100 percent. Would the coach switch back to the veteran for the biggest game of the year? No way. Belichick believed that Tom gave him the best chance to win. This would be Tom's Super Bowl to win or lose.

Many experts predicted that Belichick's choice didn't matter. New England didn't stand a chance against St. Louis, they said. But Tom and the Patriots proved the experts wrong. With less than 2 minutes to play in the game, Tom led a game-winning drive giving New England a shocking 20–17 victory.

❝*I was confident we could go out there and win the game, but you don't have to tell people that. You just have to go do it.*❞

—TOM ON HIS GAME-WINNING SUPER BOWL DRIVE

Tom was named the game's MVP and also became the youngest starting quarterback in history to win the Super Bowl (eclipsing the record of his childhood hero, Joe Montana, who had won it in 1982 at the age of 25). For Tom Brady, the future looked very bright.

Chapter | Five

In the Spotlight

Tom was an instant celebrity. He was young and good-looking. His rise to the top of the NFL from out of nowhere was an irresistible story to fans and the media. He went to Disney World, served as a judge in the Miss USA pageant, hung out with billionaire Donald Trump, and dated famous actresses and models. He was flooded with endorsement deals and media requests. It was a lot to handle. Tom's sisters Nancy and Julie moved to Boston to help their brother cope with the sudden change in lifestyle.

"I'm trying to survive," Tom said of his new celebrity status. "This is a whole new world I'm trying to live in, and I'm still trying to figure it all out."

"Tom was in vogue . . . he was the glamour boy," joked Weis of his quarterback. But behind the joke was a concern. Would Tom be able to maintain his focus in the face of all the attention?

The Patriots had become Tom's team. (New England had traded Bledsoe to the Buffalo Bills in the off-season.) Tom had a rich new contract and was headed into the season as the unquestioned starter. But what sort of expectations should fans have of him? He was a Super Bowl winner, but he hadn't even started a full season's worth of games yet.

Tom knew better than anyone that one year wasn't enough to establish himself. "The only thing I fear is not living up to my own expectations," he said. "I've seen guys who had a year of success, or three years of success, but what I'm looking for is consistency over my career. I've followed [quarterbacks] Steve Young, Joe Montana, John Elway, Dan Marino, and every year those guys were at the top."

Early on, Tom and the Pats looked ready to live up to the lofty expectations many had for them. They opened the season by trouncing the Pittsburgh Steelers 30–14. In the game, Tom completed 29 of 43 passes for 294 yards and three touchdowns. The next week, New England went on the road to face the Jets and came up with another blowout win, 44–7. Tom was accurate, and his decisions were on the mark. The Patriot offense was clicking, and Tom wasn't looking at all like a second-year starter.

In Week 3, the Pats were without a few key defensive players who were injured. New England and the Kansas City Chiefs were locked in a high-scoring shootout. Tom and the Pats' offense were moving the ball up and down the field, but the Chiefs were matching them score for score. Kansas City scored a touchdown, and they were tied 38–38.

New England won the coin toss and took the kickoff to begin overtime. Tom took control, completing a series of safe passes over the middle of the field. The big play of the drive was a 22-yard pass to Patten. After an eight-play drive, Vinatieri came on to boot the game-winning field goal. The Patriots were 3–0 on the young season. They seemed more than ready to defend their status as the league's best team.

But from there, everything began to fall apart. The team's banged-up defense wasn't shutting down opponents the way it had early in the season. Tom's inexperience seemed to catch up with him sometimes. The slide started with a 21–14 road loss to the San Diego Chargers. On first glance, Tom's numbers for the game looked good—he threw for 353 yards and two touchdowns. But he also threw two interceptions. That was rare for the young quarterback best known for taking care of the ball.

Things only got worse from there. Tom threw two more interceptions the next week in a 26–13 loss to Miami. Then he threw three picks in a 28–10 beating at the hands of the Green Bay Packers. In that game, Tom had a passer rating (a stat that measures a quarterback's overall effectiveness) of 44.0, by far the lowest of his career.

"It's embarrassing," Tom said. "It's frustrating and disappointing. It's something I haven't felt in a long time."

The Patriots fell to 3–4 after a 26–16 loss at home to the Denver Broncos. Tom didn't throw any interceptions in the game, but he didn't do much to help the offense either. He completed just 15 of 29 passes in the game for a total of 130 yards. Tom was playing poorly, and the team was in trouble.

As a team leader, Tom took the responsibility on his own shoulders to turn things around. Against Buffalo on November 3, he rediscovered his old touch. He was almost perfect on the day, completing 22 of the 26 passes he attempted for 265 yards and three touchdowns. The defense did its part, giving the Patriots a much-needed 38–7 victory to even their record at 4–4.

The team's next game, on the road against the Chicago Bears, was a wild one. The Bears weren't a very good team, but they jumped out to a 27–6 lead midway through the third quarter, largely thanks to two turnovers by Tom. Tom wasn't giving up, however. He capped a touchdown drive with a pass to running back Kevin Faulk to cut the lead to 14 points. "We were down three touchdowns, and then we scored and we're down two, and I said, 'Man, we've got a shot,'" Tom later said.

❝*Tom adopted a leadership style by which he still has time for everyone. He doesn't put himself above anybody, above the equipment manager, above the guy on the practice squad, or above a defensive player. He has respect for them doing their jobs. He gets on people, not in an overly critical way, but still firm. I don't think he's ever shown up anyone, even though some guys might deserve it.*❞

—BILL BELICHICK ON TOM'S EMERGENCE AS A TEAM LEADER

The Chicago lead was down to 11 points with a little more than five minutes to go. Tom led a drive down the field and hit Deion Branch with a 36-yard pass for a touchdown. The Patriots tried a 2-point conversion, but Faulk was unable to run the ball in, leaving the score 30–25.

The New England defense forced the Bears to punt the ball away with less than two minutes left on the clock. Tom and the offense took over at their own 44-yard line. Tom wasted no time moving the ball, hitting Patten with a 19-yard pass on the first play of the drive. Later, on a fourth-and-3 play, he kept the game alive by rushing for the first down. Then, with less than thirty seconds to go, he hit Patten in the end zone with a pass along the sideline. The officials reviewed the close play and determined that Patten had kept his feet in bounds for a touchdown. Tom later called it one of the best catches he'd ever seen. On a 2-point conversion (a 2-point play after a touchdown, rather than the usual 1-point kick), Tom hit Troy Brown with a pass to give New England a 3-point lead. The Bears couldn't do anything in the few seconds left in the game, giving New England a huge comeback victory.

❝I encourage all of my young fans to keep your bodies and minds as fit as possible and to deal with whatever challenges you may face. We never know what life is going to throw us. The best offense is to be prepared, whether for the next school test, the next game, or for an unexpected challenge.❞

—TOM BRADY

After a loss to Oakland, the Patriots put together a three-game winning streak to climb back into the playoff race. With three games to go, their record stood at 8–5. They needed to play well down the stretch to earn a playoff spot. Unfortunately for New England fans, Tom fell flat when the team needed him most. He was terrible in a 24–7 road loss to the Tennessee Titans, completing just 14 of 29 passes for 134 yards. Then at home against the Jets, he had only 133 passing yards in a 30–17 loss.

Despite the losses, the Patriots somehow entered the final week with a chance at the playoffs. If they could beat the Dolphins and the Jets lost to the Packers, they'd be in with an AFC East division title. The game was intense since the Dolphins also had a chance to make the playoffs.

Early on, Miami was in control. They built a 24–13 lead with less than five minutes to play. But then Tom came on strong, hitting Troy Brown with a 3-yard touchdown pass. The defense held after the kickoff, giving Tom and the offense the ball back. They quickly got into field-goal position, and Vinatieri came on to tie the game 24–24. Overtime!

The Patriots won the coin toss and received the kickoff. New England mixed the run and the pass to move down the field. Tom completed a big 20-yard pass to Faulk, then a 6-yarder to Brown to move the ball into field-goal range. Vinatieri came on and kicked the 35-yarder to win the game and keep New England's playoff hopes alive. Tom and his teammates celebrated, but the celebration was short-lived. The Jets dominated the Packers to claim the last remaining playoff spot and end New England's season. The Pats had finished with a winning record, 9–7, but it was a bitterly disappointing ending for the defending champs.

"I feel tired," Tom said when it was all over. "It's been a long year and obviously we played so late last season. These weeks go on and on and I think you're just like playing on the vapor with [no] gas left. . . . To kind of dig deep like we did, obviously that shows what kind of character we have."

Tom had finished the season with 3,764 passing yards for twenty-eight touchdowns and fourteen interceptions. They were decent numbers, but he had sputtered down the stretch and had, at times, looked like he'd taken a step back from his 2001 season. Many fans wondered, was Tom's 2001 success a fluke? Or would he be able to prove that he was more than a one-shot wonder? The 2003 season would tell the story.

Chapter Six

Back on Top

Tom had separated his shoulder in the final game of the season, and the team had kept it quiet. He could have had surgery but chose not to. So Tom spent the off-season rehabbing, hoping he'd be ready for the start of the season.

Tom's health was one of several questions facing the Patriots entering the 2003 season. One of the team's best defensive players, Lawyer Milloy, was gone. Aside from Tom, the team didn't really have any bona fide NFL superstars. Had the 2001 Patriots been a fluke? Or could Tom and his teammates prove that they had the skills to get back to the top?

The early indications were not good. New England opened the season in Buffalo to face the Bills. The game held a little extra drama since both Bledsoe and Milloy were playing for the Bills. The two former Pats led a complete dismantling of New England. Buffalo scored early and often, and Tom and the New

England offense looked terrible. Buffalo took a 21–0 lead into halftime, helped by an interception Tom had thrown for a Bills touchdown in the second quarter. Things didn't get any better in the second half, and the Patriots walked off the field embarrassed, on the bad side of a 31–0 blowout.

But in Week 2, Tom and his teammates bounced back. He threw three touchdown passes in a 31–10 victory over a good Philadelphia Eagles team. Then New England beat the Jets 23–16.

A loss to the Washington Redskins dropped New England's record to 2–2. Beginning in Week 5, in a 38–30 win over Tennessee, New England caught fire. The defense was playing great, and Tom and the offense were moving the ball and putting points on the board. Few of the victories were blowouts. But the Patriots were finding ways to win every close game.

In one game, New England and Miami were tied 13–13 in overtime. The Dolphins had several chances to win, but they missed field goals, keeping New England alive. Finally, Tom took advantage of the Dolphins' mistakes. From his own 18-yard line, he took the snap and dropped back. He saw Troy Brown streaking across the field, running a route called a slant. Tom fired a pass to the sprinting Brown, who caught it between two defenders and raced to the end zone for the game-winning touchdown.

"It was unbelievable," Tom said of the play. "We were down and out a few times. The offensive line gave me a lot of time. I let it go and [Brown] made a great catch. This shows the mental toughness this team has. We made the adjustments and we're only going to get better."

66[Tom's] got a doctorate in defensive football. He understands what [defenses are] doing and, if they're not doing it, why they're vulnerable. That's what Tom's great at. He understands how a defense should be played.99

—BILL BELICHICK

Tom continued to lift his team. The winning streak went on and on. With one game to go, the Patriots were 13–2 and had clinched a playoff spot.

The Patriots needed a win in the last game to secure the top seed (ranking) in the AFC playoffs, which would mean home-field advantage. But that wasn't the only reason they wanted to do well. Their opponent, the Buffalo Bills, had handed them an embarrassing loss in the season's first game. New England wanted to settle the score.

They did exactly that. In the first quarter, Tom threw two touchdown passes. He threw two more in the second quarter. The Patriot defense shut down Bledsoe and the Bills, and by the end, the Patriots had their revenge, 31–0. They'd clinched the top seed and had knocked Buffalo out of the playoffs in the process. "We proved we were a different team than that first day," Tom told reporters.

A FLATTERING COMPARISON

By late 2003, some fans and media were suggesting that Tom had a lot in common with the young Joe Montana. Tom was honored by the comparison, but he also made sure people knew he didn't believe in it. "[Montana is] the best of all time," Tom said. "Everything that he did was great. He managed his game great. He threw the ball great. He made his other players great. . . . Do I think I have any of those great qualities? I'm working at it. I'm working to try to become that, but it's going to . . . take a lot more Super Bowl wins to ever mention those two names in the same sentence."

With the top seed, New England had a bye in the first round. In the divisional round, they faced the league co-MVP Steve McNair and the Titans, who had beaten the Baltimore Ravens in the first round. Tennessee was a defense-oriented team well suited to the Patriots' tough style of football. As expected, the game was close and hard-fought. It was a bitterly cold day, with windchills dipping to –11 degrees Fahrenheit.

Tom could see his own breath as he barked out signals from behind the center.

The Patriots opened the scoring in the first quarter. Tom spotted receiver Bethel Johnson dashing down the middle of the field. He heaved a perfect pass, and Johnson sprinted to the end zone for a 7–0 lead. The Titans came back to tie the game 7–7 and again, later, at 14–14. In the fourth quarter, Vinatieri missed a kick that would have put the Patriots ahead, but Tom gave him another chance. With just over four minutes left in the game, the New England kicker booted one just over the crossbar for a 17–14 lead. The New England defense held, and the Patriots won yet another close game—their thirteenth win in a row.

Next up was the AFC Championship against the powerful Indianapolis Colts. The Colts featured a potent offense led by quarterback Peyton Manning, the other co-MVP. A rivalry was beginning to brew between the two teams. Many experts considered Manning to be the game's best young quarterback—a title to which Patriot fans thought Tom also had a claim.

Tom made his case on the field. He and the Patriot offense executed a grueling, time-consuming, thirteen-play, 65-yard drive that ended with a touchdown pass to Givens. Manning and the Colts appeared ready to answer back, driving the ball all the way down to the 7-yard line, but New England safety Rodney Harrison picked off one of Manning's passes in the end zone.

Tom *(left)* tries to tag out a runner at the plate while playing catcher for the Junipero Serra High School baseball team.

Tom leads the Michigan Wolverines in the 2000 Orange Bowl. The Wolverines beat Alabama 35–34.

Tom warms up on the sidelines during his rookie season with the Patriots in 2000.

Tom led the Patriots to a win over the Oakland Raiders during a snowy AFC divisional playoff game in 2002.

Tom evades a tackle during Super Bowl XXXVI in 2002. The Patriots beat the St. Louis Rams 20–17.

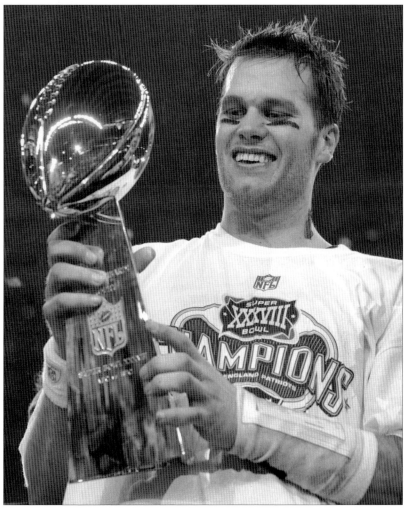

Tom holds the Vince Lombardi Trophy after winning Super Bowl XXXVIII in 2004.

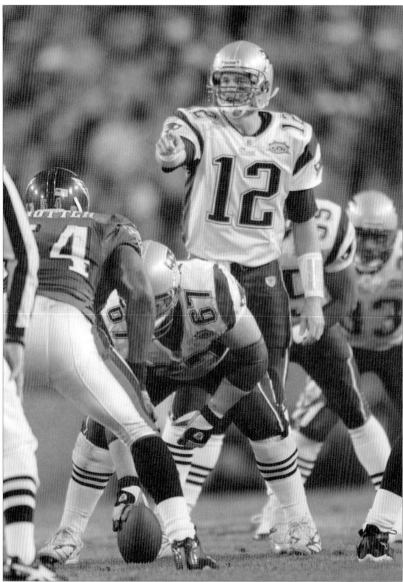

Tom makes a change at the line of scrimmage during Super Bowl XXXIX in 2005.

Tom throws a touchdown pass to Randy Moss in the final game of the 2007 regular season. The pass was Tom's fiftieth of the season, an NFL record. On the play, Moss also broke an NFL record with twenty-three receiving touchdowns.

In 2007, Tom had a son, John Edward Thomas Moynahan, with Bridget Moynahan *(right)*.

Tom married Gisele Bündchen in early 2009.

The defenses took over from there. New England managed two field goals and a safety in the second quarter, while Manning and the Colts couldn't put any points on the board. Tom and the Patriots nursed that lead in the second half, adding three more field goals. Manning and the Indy offense finally broke through in the second half with two touchdowns, but these points weren't nearly enough. Tom and the Patriots had a 24–14 victory—their fourteenth win in a row—and were headed back to the Super Bowl.

"To win fourteen in a row, that's unbelievable," Tom said. "I mean, who does that? Nobody does that, and it's great will and great determination. . . . And still the goal really hasn't been achieved, so winning fourteen in a row is great, but if there is not a fifteenth, then it's all for nothing."

Tom had been there before, but this time around, the Super Bowl hype felt different. "I think I have somewhat of an idea what I'm getting into this time," he said. "It got so chaotic two years ago, I found myself thinking, 'When is this season going to end?' I don't feel that way this time."

Tom and his teammates took the field with confidence. Their opponent was the surprising Carolina Panthers, who had gone 11–5 in the regular season. At first, the contest looked like it would be a defensive battle. Neither team scored in the first quarter. As the second quarter dragged on, the score remained knotted at zeros.

Late in the quarter, the Patriots got the ball in great field position after recovering a Panther fumble. But Tom and his offense were facing a tough third-and-7 play. If they couldn't pick up 7 yards, they'd have to try kicking a field goal, and they'd already missed two field-goal tries in the half. Tom took the snap and dropped back, scanning the field for an open receiver. He couldn't find one. As the Carolina pass rush closed in, Tom took off with the ball, scrambling up the middle to pick up 12 yards and a first down. On this rare occasion, Tom used his legs, rather than his arm, to make a big play. On the next play, Tom cashed in with a 5-yard touchdown pass to Branch to give New England a 7–0 lead.

Two minutes later, the Panthers answered with a touchdown of their own. Tom and the Patriots got the ball back with just a minute to go in the half. But instead of playing it safe, Belichick let his quarterback play aggressively. From the shotgun formation, in which the quarterback starts several yards behind the line, Tom completed a 12-yard pass to Givens. Then he rifled a pass 42 yards downfield to Branch, who caught the ball and ran for another 10 yards before being tackled. Two plays later, Tom found Givens open in the end zone. He'd led the Pats down the field in less than forty seconds! In fact, he may have scored too quickly because the Panthers had enough time to set up a field goal to pull within 14–10 as the half expired. After scoring no points in the first 26 minutes, 55 seconds, of the half, the teams had exploded for a combined 24 points in the final 3:05!

The thrilling end to the first half set the tone for a dramatic second half. Neither team scored in the third quarter. Then, in the fourth quarter, both teams poured it on. New England extended their lead to 21–10 on an Antowain Smith touchdown run. The Panthers quickly answered back with a touchdown of their own. They went for a 2-point conversion, which failed, leaving the score 21–16.

On the next drive, Tom led his team down to Carolina's 9-yard line. But on a third-down play, he tried to do too much and threw an interception to Carolina's Reggie Howard. Four plays later, Carolina quarterback Jake Delhomme capitalized on Tom's mistake, hitting receiver Muhsin Muhammad with a stunning 85-yard touchdown pass. The big play, with another missed 2-point conversion, gave Carolina a 22–21 lead with just under seven minutes to go.

Tom later insisted that the big turn of events didn't rattle him. "That's what happens in the Super Bowl, you know?" he said. "They make great plays too."

Tom had his turn again to make great plays. He led the Patriots on another long drive. Highlighted by an 18-yard pass to Givens on a third-and-9 play, the Patriots reclaimed the lead with a 1-yard touchdown pass to Mike Vrabel. The touchdown gave the Patriots a 27–22 lead, so they went for a 2-point conversion to extend the lead to 7. Running back Kevin Faulk carried the ball in for the conversion—29–22.

Less than three minutes remained, but Carolina wasn't done. Delhomme answered back once again, throwing a game-tying touchdown pass to receiver Ricky Proehl with just over a minute left in the game.

This was good news and bad news for the Panthers. The good news was that they'd tied the game. The bad news was that they'd left Tom far too much time on the clock. Tom used that time, calmly driving the Patriots down the field with big passes to Brown and Branch.

With 9 seconds to go, Tom's job was complete. The ball was at Carolina's 23-yard line, which gave Vinatieri a relatively easy 41-yard field-goal attempt. Tom watched from the sideline as Vinatieri calmly kicked the ball through the uprights. The Patriots had done it! They were the Super Bowl champions for the second time in three years! The legend of Tom Brady was growing.

 Tom was voted the Super Bowl MVP for his performance. He had completed 32 of 48 passes for 323 yards and three touchdowns.

Chapter Seven

Repeat

After his first Super Bowl victory, Tom had soaked up the attention. After his second one, he tried to stay out of the spotlight. He spent some time recovering from minor surgery. He also took a three-week vacation with his new girlfriend, model and actress Bridget Moynahan. "[Tom has] kept a low profile," said Patriots owner Robert Kraft. "The first time, he was like a little kid . . . reacting to everything that came at him. This time, having been through the process, he's much more prepared. He's managing his life this time, instead of other people managing his life."

❝[Tom] has no interest in being a celebrity, but he knows he is one. He just makes sure it doesn't get in the way of his life.❞

—TOM'S DAD

Tom was focused on the 2004 season. The Patriots were well positioned to defend their Super Bowl title. The NFL is famous for its parity. That means that often the same teams have a hard time being good year after year. Every team has a chance to compete, and feats like winning back-to-back Super Bowls are rare accomplishments. With constant player and coach movement around the league, the threat of injuries, and the overall quality of competition, building a dynasty is very difficult. But entering the 2004 season, that's exactly what Tom, Belichick, and the Patriots were looking to accomplish.

The season opened with a much-anticipated AFC Championship rematch against the Colts. The Brady-Manning rivalry was hotter than ever. Both quarterbacks had nothing but kind words for each other, and they were always eager to be at their best when playing. This was a matchup between the NFL's two premiere quarterbacks and the AFC's two best teams.

The Colts took a halftime lead of 17–13. In the second half, Tom took over. He thrilled the New England crowd by throwing two third-quarter touchdown passes, including a 25-yard strike to Patten. The New England defense made the lead hold up, and the 27–24 final score extended the Pats' overall winning streak to sixteen games (including their final twelve games of 2003 and three playoff games). In the game, Tom threw for three touchdowns and 335 yards on 26–38 passing.

The winning streak just grew and grew. New England seemed unstoppable, racking up road wins in Arizona and Buffalo. The Patriots were in uncharted territory—no NFL team had ever won so many games in a row. Even when Tom wasn't at his best, they seemed to win with ease. That was true on October 10, when New England handily beat the Dolphins despite two interceptions and only 76 yards passing out of Tom. If the offense had an off game, the defense picked up the slack. When the defense struggled, the offense did enough to win the game.

Several big challenges lay ahead. One of them was a game against the Seattle Seahawks on October 17—a matchup many fans thought could be a Super Bowl preview. The Patriots didn't blink, however, and easily handled one of the best teams the National Football Conference (NFC) had to offer. They built an early 17–0 lead and never looked back. A week later, New England held on to a tight victory over the Jets, 13–7, to set up a trip to Pittsburgh to play a very good Steelers team.

The Patriots opened the scoring with a field goal, but the game was a disaster after that. The Steelers roared up and down the field. They harassed Tom into two costly turnovers and built a big lead early. By the final whistle, Pittsburgh had a convincing 34–20 victory, and the Patriots' long streak was finally over. Belichick was hard on himself and on his team. "[Pittsburgh] outcoached us. They outplayed us. We were not very good in any phase of the game. We did not do much right."

The Patriots weren't used to failure, and they didn't often experience the feeling for the rest of the season. The next week, Tom and his teammates went back to work to build a new winning streak. There was no letdown as New England easily handled a good Rams team in St. Louis. Tom threw two touchdown passes and Patriot running back Corey Dillon ran over the Rams' defense in a 40–22 pounding that moved New England's record to 7–1.

The new winning streak was on. The Patriots went on to win six games in a row to move to 12–1. They had the AFC East wrapped up when they lost again, a surprising 29–28 defeat against a poor Dolphins team on *Monday Night Football*. With two more victories to finish the season, the Patriots were 14–2 and the number-two seed in the AFC playoffs.

After a first-round bye, the Patriots faced a familiar foe in the Colts. Peyton Manning was coming off of a fantastic season that had earned him the NFL's MVP award, and the Indy offense had looked, at times, virtually unstoppable. But the Patriots had the Colts' number, especially at home. As good as Manning was against the rest of the league, he consistently struggled against New England. This time around was no different. The Patriots' defense was the story. They swarmed all over the field, confusing and frustrating Manning and the Colts. Tom threw for one touchdown and ran in another himself as the Patriots dominated the Colts 20–3. Indy coach Tony Dungy gave the Patriots all the credit. "We just ran into a better team today," he said. "That's one thing about them. They find a way to win." Tom had just played the seventh playoff game of his career. His record: an amazing 7–0.

That spotless record would be put to a huge test in the AFC Championship. The Patriots squared off once more with the Pittsburgh Steelers, a team that had finished the season 15–1 and, counting their playoff win over the Jets, was on a fifteen-game winning streak. Tom and his teammates knew they'd have their hands full with a tough opponent and a rowdy Pittsburgh crowd. After all, the Steelers had been the team to break New England's long winning streak earlier that season.

Tom and his teammates didn't take long to silence the Pittsburgh crowd, however. They opened the scoring with a field goal, then the New England defense forced a fumble. Tom wanted to capitalize on the situation right away. He dropped back on the first play of the drive and rifled a pass to Branch. Branch took it 60 yards to the end zone to put New England ahead 10–0. By halftime, that lead had grown to 24–3, and the Pittsburgh fans were actually booing their own team off the field. The Patriots kept rolling in the second half, punching their tickets to a third Super Bowl in four years with a 41–27 beat-down. In the game, Tom threw for 207 yards and two touchdowns.

As usual, Tom didn't want to talk about his own performance but that of the team. "This team has a lot of grit," he told reporters. "We just kept answering the bell."

Could anyone stop the Patriots? Many experts didn't think so. The AFC conference was by far the more dominant in the NFL. The NFC's Super Bowl representative, the Philadelphia Eagles, had finished the regular season 13–3. They were built around a strong defense and quarterback Donovan McNabb. Still, most experts expected the Patriots to easily handle the Eagles in the Super Bowl. But if Patriots fans were expecting an easy victory, they were in for a disappointment.

Both defenses came out strong, leading to a scoreless first quarter. Early in the second quarter, Philadelphia broke through with a touchdown. Tom and the Patriots answered back, driving down to the Eagles' 40-yard line with about a minute to go before halftime. On second down, Tom looked right, then scanned the middle of the field, trying to find an open receiver. The Eagle pass rush was storming in quickly—he had to make a decision. Then Tom noticed Givens in the far right corner of the end zone. Tom was on the move, so he wouldn't be able to set his body to make the throw with his usual accuracy. He threw the ball sidearm toward Givens. Tom knew the pass had to be perfect—anything less would be risking a costly interception.

"Tom threw it right where he had to throw it," Givens said. "I looked up and it hit me exactly where I wanted it. Tom placed the ball right on the money."

The thrilling touchdown pass sent the teams into the locker room tied 7–7. In the second half, Tom picked up right where he'd left off, leading a long New England drive. He hit Branch on pass after pass to move down the field. Finally, he capped the drive with a short touchdown pass to Vrabel.

The Eagles quickly bounced back with a touchdown of their own. But they couldn't keep pace with Tom and the Pats' offense. Once again, Tom led a long drive that ended in a Dillon touchdown. Yet another drive resulted in a field goal and a 10-point lead.

The Eagles frantically tried to come back, cutting the margin to 3 points. But the New England defense stepped up and stopped the scoring there. Tom took the final snap and dropped to a knee to run the final seconds off the clock. The Patriots had done it! They'd won their third Super Bowl title in four years.

❝*I felt I was very prepared tonight, more so than ever before. I wish we had gotten things going a little quicker, but I knew I was looking in the right places.*❞

—TOM ON HIS SUPER BOWL PERFORMANCE

Tom finished the game having completed 23 of 33 passes for 236 yards and two touchdowns. The MVP honors went to Branch, who caught a record-tying eleven passes.

 Tom wasn't able to enjoy his third Super Bowl victory as much as his first two. A few days before the big game, his grandmother passed away.

"The Eagles were tough," Tom told reporters. "But we had the determination. We fought hard for 60 minutes and came out the champs. It really hasn't sunk in yet and I don't think it's going to sink in for a while." Media members asked if New England could officially be called an NFL dynasty. "We've never really self-proclaimed ourselves anything," Tom answered. "If you guys say we're great, we'll accept the compliment."

At age 27, Tom was a three-time Super Bowl champion. The NFL had never seen anyone meet with so much success so soon. The Patriots were the undisputed powerhouse of the NFL. How much longer could they hold on to that title?

Chapter | Eight

Disappointments

The amazing start to Tom's NFL career was going to be tough to live up to. The 28-year-old quarterback had played in nine career playoff games, and he had won all of them. To many, reaching the playoffs seemed almost a given, and, once there, the Pats were expected to dominate. Anything short of another Super Bowl run in the 2005 season would be seen as a failure.

Things in New England were changing, however. The Patriots were winners, and everybody wants a piece of a winner. Offensive coordinator Charlie Weis left the team to take a college coaching job. Defensive coordinator Romeo Crennel also moved on, as did several key players, including Ty Law.

"This will be our most challenging year," Tom said. "You want . . . to be at a championship level. My job as the quarterback is to make sure not that we're better than last year, but that we are the best we can be this year."

Before the 2005 season, Tom signed a contract extension with the Patriots. His new contract paid him $60 million over six years.

The 2005 season started out well, with a 30–20 victory over the Raiders in which Tom threw for 306 yards and two touchdowns. Then Carolina handed the defending champs a 27–17 loss in Week 2. This pattern—win a game, lose a game—continued through the first ten games of the season. Remarkably, the Pats didn't win consecutive games until Weeks 10 and 11 of the season—23–16 over the Dolphins and 24–17 over the Saints.

Could the team ride the momentum of their first winning streak of the year? They traveled to Kansas City to find out. The answer was a resounding no. The Chiefs jumped all over the Patriots. Tom played horribly. He threw four interceptions in the game—three of them to one player—and the Patriots quickly fell behind. They trailed in the game 26–3 before a few late scores made the final score, 26–16, look more respectable.

"Tough day," Tom said. "We didn't execute. It's tough when you spot a good team all those points. I just threw it high."

The loss dropped the Patriots to 6–5 on the season and put them in serious danger of missing the playoffs. They had five games to go and would have to win at least three to earn a play-off spot. But the Patriots were the champs for a reason, and they came through in crunch time. Over the next three weeks, they outscored their competition by a total of 79–10. The highlight for Tom came in the third of those games, a 28–0 victory over a good Tampa Bay Buccaneers team in which he threw three touchdown passes. The victory gave New England the AFC East title, securing their spot in the playoffs.

PLAYING WITH PAIN

Sometime during the middle of the 2005 season, Tom suffered an injury called a sports hernia. This tearing of the stomach wall was painful and limited Tom's ability to move around quickly in the pocket. But he played through the pain, waiting to have surgery until after the season was over.

The team split its final two games to finish the season 10–6. Tom barely played in the season finale, a loss to the Dolphins, because Belichick wanted to keep him fresh for the playoffs. Unlike in past years, New England was not one of the top two teams in the conference, so they had to play in the Wild Card round. Their opponent was the Jacksonville Jaguars, who had finished the regular season at an impressive 12–4. But even though Jacksonville had the better record, the Patriots played at home because they had won their division while the Jags had finished second in theirs.

On paper, it looked like a great matchup. On the field, however, the Patriots looked like they were in another league. The New England defense stifled the Jacksonville offense, while Tom was in his usual playoff form. He threw three touchdown passes and made virtually no mistakes in the 28–3 blowout. The win made Tom ten for ten in playoff games in his career. New England's ten straight playoff victories was an NFL record.

Tom wasn't satisfied, however. "We're going to keep fighting, I know we will keep fighting," he said. "We'll get ready to play the toughest game of the year. Now we are even with the best teams in the league, Indy and Denver."

One of those two teams—Denver—was waiting. The Broncos had used a good offense and a dominating defense to build a 13–3 regular-season record. But the team didn't come close to matching New England in terms of playoff experience. Could the Patriots use that experience to their advantage?

Denver came out strong, building a 10–3 halftime lead. Tom and the Patriot offense cut that lead to 10–6 with a field goal early in the third quarter. Then they got the ball back again with a chance to take a lead. Tom started the drive with a 33-yard pass to Brown, followed by a 26-yard pass to Branch. He was looking like the confident, mistake-free quarterback who had won three Super Bowls. Soon, the Patriots were at the Denver 5-yard line. On third down, Tom took the snap and fired a quick pass in the direction of Brown. But Denver cornerback Champ Bailey stepped in front of the pass, intercepting it in the end zone. Bailey darted out of the end zone and started streaking down the field. A touchdown seemed sure, but Patriot tight end Ben Watson caught Bailey and knocked the ball out of his hands. The ball sailed out of bounds near the end zone. The officials ruled that it was Denver's ball at the 1-yard line. On the next play, Broncos running back Mike Anderson finished it off with a touchdown run, all but putting the game away.

Tom took his first playoff loss hard. "When you lose, you want to go down fighting," he told reporters. "You want to go down playing your best and we didn't do that. We made it easy for them."

A rare bit of controversy touched Tom in August 2006. A report linked him to Greg Anderson, a trainer who was under investigation in a steroids scandal. At the center of the scandal was baseball star Barry Bonds, who had gone to the same high school as Tom. Tom insisted that he had contacted Anderson only once, about working out when he was going to be back home, but he had never even met Anderson. There was no evidence to suggest Tom was using or had ever used any banned substances.

The 2006 season was one of change for the Patriots offense. Receivers Givens and Branch left the team, as did Vinatieri. New additions included running back Lawrence Maroney, the team's first-round pick, and rookie kicker Stephen Gostkowski. Not surprisingly, with the offense in flux, the New England defense came up big in the season opener against Buffalo.

The game started out terribly for Tom. On the Patriots' first offensive play, he fumbled as Buffalo defenders converged on him in the pocket. The Bills dominated the first half, building a 17–7 lead. But Tom and the offense stormed back to tie the game 17–17, highlighted by a 93-yard drive that ended in a touchdown pass from Tom to Kevin Faulk. Late in the fourth quarter, Buffalo had the ball deep in their own territory. From the 8-yard line, Buffalo quarterback J. P. Losman took the snap and dropped back. The Pats' defense charged, forcing Losman to scramble. But before he could get rid of the ball, defensive end Ty Warren drove him to the ground in the end zone for a safety. The 2-point safety gave the Patriots a 19–17 lead, which they held on to for a big win.

After beating the Jets 24–17, the Patriots had a rematch at home with Denver, the team that had knocked them out of the playoffs in the previous season. The Patriots' fans were eager for revenge, but once again the Broncos were the better team. Tom couldn't get anything going against the stout Denver defense. It was 17–0 Denver by the fourth quarter, and a late touchdown pass was far too little, too late.

FEELING CHARITABLE

Tom has always been eager to give back. He gives both time and money to a variety of causes. Helping kids around the world is among his greatest passions. He has worked with a group that helps to provide laptop computers for underprivileged children and has traveled to Africa to fight hunger and poverty.

New England regrouped, winning its next four games. The highlight of the streak was a Monday night game against the Minnesota Vikings. The Vikings had, by far, the best running defense in the league. So rather than try to run against them, Belichick decided that the Patriots would just pass. And pass. And pass. Tom was on fire, hitting receiver after receiver, racking up 372 passing yards and four touchdown passes in a 31–7 victory.

Tom was all smiles after the game. "The plan was to come out and put the ball in the air a little bit," he said. "The receivers made a lot of great plays, and it was a lot of fun, needless to say."

As good as Tom had been against Minnesota, he was awful the next week against the rival Colts. He threw four interceptions against a Colts defense that many considered weak. The Patriots played hard, but in the end they couldn't overcome all of the mistakes. The Colts won the game 27–20 to drop New England's season record to 6–2. The Pats lost again the next week before catching fire. New England won six of its last seven games—including another four-touchdown performance from Tom in a 35–0 win over the Green Bay Packers—to win the AFC East with an 11–5 record. On the season, Tom completed 319 of 516 passes for 3,529 yards and 24 touchdowns.

Tom's life changed in another way late in 2006. He and girlfriend Bridget Moynahan stopped dating. The couple wanted different things, according to reports. Moynahan was six years older than Tom and wanted to start a family, whereas Tom wanted to focus on football. In addition, Tom had a new love interest, Brazilian supermodel Gisele Bündchen. But shortly after their breakup, Moynahan told Tom that she was pregnant with his baby. The news was hard for Tom to cope with and became a big controversy. Not only had he fathered a child out of wedlock, he was already dating someone else. Tom, who had been raised Catholic, took a lot of criticism for these events. People said he was an irresponsible womanizer. It was a difficult time for Tom, who prefers to keep his private life private. The baby was due in the summer. For the time being, Tom would remain focused on football.

In August 2007, Tom was at the hospital for the birth of his first child, a son. The baby's name was John Edward Thomas Moynahan. The media quickly adopted the nickname "JET" for the baby, taking his first three initials and using them to spell the team nickname of one of New England's biggest rivals—the New York Jets.

The Patriots' 11–5 record wasn't good enough to earn them a first-round bye, so they hosted a playoff game against the Jets. The game was a complete mismatch. Tom and the Patriots dominated in a 37–16 victory that was never really in doubt. That set up a contest against the powerful San Diego Chargers.

The game was not a thing of beauty. Both teams made serious mistakes, including three interceptions from Tom. On one of the interceptions, however, the Chargers fumbled the ball right back to New England. Tom took advantage of the second chance by finding Reche Caldwell in the end zone for a touchdown. After a successful 2-point conversion, the game was tied 21–21.

That's where the score stood with just over three minutes to play. The Patriots had the ball at their own 15-yard line. Tom calmly led the team down the field. The big play of the drive came on third-and-10. If the Patriots couldn't convert the first down, the Chargers would have an outstanding chance to drive for a game-winning score. Tom dropped back and scanned the field. He found Caldwell and hit him with a 49-yard pass play that took the Patriots into field-goal range. Gostkowski booted the 31-yard field goal to give the Patriots a 24–21 lead. When the Chargers were unable to answer on their next drive, the game was over. A relieved Tom turned to linebacker Tedy Bruschi and said, "Man, that was not easy." "They never are, buddy. They never are," Bruschi replied.

❝When you are a kid, everyone wants to grow up and play sports. You want to succeed. But there are still times when I sit around with my mom and my dad and say, 'Can you believe this?'**❞**

—TOM BRADY

The Patriots were riding high, and they rode that momentum into Indianapolis, where they faced the Colts in the AFC Championship. The Patriots jumped all over the Colts in the first half, scoring two defensive touchdowns and building an early 21–3 lead. Colts fans had seen their team lose to New England time and again in the playoffs, and this game looked no different.

But everything changed in the second half. Manning caught fire. He led the Colts back to a 21–21 tie. Then Tom threw a touchdown pass to receiver Jabar Gaffney to reclaim the lead, but Manning wasn't done. Soon, the game was tied 31–31. Only a few minutes remained in regulation. Tom and the Patriots' offense kept fighting, driving into Gostkowski's field-goal range. The rookie kicker did his part, splitting the uprights to give the Patriots a 34–31 lead with just over three minutes to play.

Then Manning had his turn. He completed pass after pass to get the Colts into field-goal range. But Indy didn't settle for the tie. Running back Joseph Addai punched the ball into the end zone for a 38–34 lead. Just a minute remained on the clock. Tom tried to lead the Patriots back, but he was intercepted on a late desperation pass. The Patriots watched in shock as the Colts celebrated. Once again, New England would be watching the Super Bowl from home.

A disappointed Tom spoke to reporters after the game. "Do I think I had a great season? I mean I think it's always judged on whether you win the Super Bowl or not. I mean we're in the AFC Championship, coming down the fourth quarter with the lead. You're three and a half minutes from winning the AFC Championship, so . . . You just try to take what you learned and move on and try to do it better next year."

For any other team—and any other quarterback—being one win away from the Super Bowl might be a great season. But this wasn't any team, and this wasn't any quarterback. Tom and the Patriots had something to prove.

Chapter Nine

Perfection?

The Patriots' offense got a face-lift before the 2007 season. First, New England added receivers Donté Stallworth and Wes Welker. Those moves alone would have been enough to provide a big boost to their passing game. But the Patriots didn't stop there. Star receiver Randy Moss had just finished two disappointing seasons in Oakland. He was unhappy in Oakland, and the struggling Raiders were willing to trade him for a draft pick. The Patriots made the move.

Adding Moss would instantly give the offense an explosiveness it had never really possessed. But the trade remained controversial. Moss had been labeled a selfish player by many in the media, despite the fact that his teammates often said that he was misunderstood. Still, many claimed that Moss was not a good fit for the Patriots and their team-first approach. However, nobody was more excited about the addition than Tom. In fact,

Tom restructured his contract to make sure the Patriots had enough salary cap space to add the high-priced receiver.

"I'm still overwhelmed and, at the same time, kind of star-struck that I am part of this New England Patriots organization," Moss said. "I've always been a big fan of Tom Brady's. I talked to Tom Brady today, just to jump some things off and just let him know how excited I am to play with him and also the other players on this team."

RANDY MOSS

Randy Moss is one of the NFL's all-time greatest and most controversial wide receivers. Born on February 13, 1977, in West Virginia, he was a star football and basketball player in high school. He attended Marshall University, and the Minnesota Vikings selected him in the first round of the 1998 draft. Moss set the NFL on fire, catching 17 touchdown passes in his rookie year. He starred for the Vikings through 2004, when off-the-field troubles forced them to trade him to Oakland. After two lackluster seasons, Moss moved on to New England, where he once again became one of the most dangerous players in the game.

Tom had never had a corps of receivers so dangerous, and he wasn't about to waste the opportunity. In the Patriots' opener, on the road against the Jets, Tom used his new receivers early and often. He started with an 11-yard touchdown pass to Welker in the first quarter. But Moss was clearly Tom's new favorite target. Moss caught nine passes for 183 yards, including a thrilling 51-yard bomb for a touchdown, as the Patriots rolled to a 38–14 victory.

The win was a great start, but unfortunately, what most NFL fans remembered about that game wasn't the Brady-to-Moss connection. It was what came after—accusations that the Patriots had cheated. The NFL had evidence that Belichick's staff had been illegally taping the New York sideline during the game to steal defensive signals. The fallout was severe. Accusations flew that Belichick and the Pats had been cheating for years. (The Rams suspected them of doing so in a Super Bowl.) The NFL fined both Belichick and the team and stripped the team of its 2008 first-round draft pick. The Patriots also knew that they'd be playing under a microscope for the rest of the season.

As if they had something to prove, Tom and the Patriots came out stronger than ever the next week. Their opponent, the San Diego Chargers, was considered one of the best teams in the league. But they didn't look like it. Once again, Tom and the Patriots were unstoppable. Tom threw three touchdown passes in the game, including two more to Moss, and the Patriots won once again, by a score of 38–14. "After everything that went on this week, we wanted to do our best for [Belichick]," Tom told reporters after the game.

New England's magic number seemed to be 38 because that's how many points they scored again—for the third week in a row—in a 38–7 rout of the Bills. Tom threw four touchdown passes in the game, giving him a remarkable ten touchdowns through just three games.

The wins and the touchdown passes just kept coming. Tom threw three touchdowns in each of the next two games, a 34–13 trouncing of Cincinnati and a 34–17 win over the Cleveland Browns.

The 5–0 Patriots were set for a big matchup with the Dallas Cowboys, who were also 5–0. Many billed the game as a possible Super Bowl preview. If any team could keep up with the Patriots, the Dallas Cowboys could, experts said.

But even at home, the Cowboys were hopelessly overmatched. First-quarter touchdown passes to Moss and Welker put the Patriots up, and they never looked back. Tom was cool, collected, and deadly accurate in the pocket, completing 31 of 46 passes for 388 yards and a remarkable five touchdown passes. When the Patriots added a 1-yard touchdown run with just 19 seconds to go, the score was an embarrassing 48–27. It was the most points a Patriot team had scored in 23 years.

The last touchdown was an example of how Belichick had been running up the score late in blowouts. An unwritten NFL rule says that teams should not score unnecessarily in blowout wins. It's a courtesy not to embarrass your opponent. But Belichick was gaining a reputation for ignoring that unwritten rule. He didn't care what the score was; he wanted to keep scoring. Some reporters suggested that upping the score was his way of answering all of the criticism he'd received as a result of the cheating scandal. But his decision didn't make him any more popular with his peers.

Through six games, Tom had 21 touchdown passes. No quarterback in NFL history had thrown so many through the first six games. That meant that Tom was on a pace to break Peyton Manning's NFL record of 49 touchdown passes in a season. But when asked about his record pace, Tom told reporters he didn't want to talk about records. "That's not what this team is about," he said. "Individual records are based on opportunities. What I get excited about is team records."

But talk about a possible record only got louder the next week. In a 49–28 thrashing of the Dolphins, Tom did himself one better, throwing for a jaw-dropping six touchdowns, including five in the first half alone! He orchestrated a merciless aerial assault that the Dolphins were powerless to stop. "[My receivers] are making the plays," said a humble Tom after the game. "I'm just throwing it. They're making my job awful easy."

Suddenly, Manning's touchdown record didn't seem like the only one in jeopardy. Moss was on pace to set a new receiving touchdowns record. The Patriots' offense was on pace to challenge the record of the 1998 Vikings for most points scored in a season (another team that had featured Randy Moss). And perhaps most important, they were starting to look like they could go undefeated in the regular season—a feat accomplished only by the 1972 Miami Dolphins, who had gone 14–0 in the regular season before winning all their playoff games and the Super Bowl.

After a 52–7 pasting of the Washington Redskins, the Patriots were 8–0, and NFL fans were salivating over the next game on the schedule. New England traveled to Indianapolis to face the Colts—who were also undefeated at 7–0—in a matchup that the media was calling the game of the century. Never in NFL history had two undefeated teams squared off so late in the season. Which team would emerge as the dominant force in the AFC?

Unlike most of New England's games in 2007, this one was no blowout. The teams appeared evenly matched. The Colts scored first and took a 13–7 lead into halftime. A Manning touchdown early in the fourth quarter extended the Indy lead to 20–10. Tom and his teammates never blinked. "There wasn't any loss of confidence or determination," Tom said after the game.

Cool as ever, Tom took the field. He hit Moss with two long passes, then connected with Welker for a touchdown. The New

England defense did its part, forcing an Indianapolis punt. Once again, Tom took over. Three plays—and three passes—later, Tom hit Faulk in the end zone for the touchdown and a 24–20 lead. The defense made the score hold up, and the Patriots moved to 9–0 on the season.

❝*[Peyton Manning has] probably got a better arm. He's faster. He's bigger. He's probably smarter. He's proven over the years how consistent he is. I've always looked up to Peyton and the way he plays.*❞

—TOM, COMPARING HIMSELF TO PEYTON MANNING

The Patriots looked unstoppable as they kept winning. A few games were close, including 3-point victories over Philadelphia and Baltimore, but for the most part, nobody could keep up. The winning streak grew to twelve games, then fourteen. A 28–7 victory over the Miami Dolphins brought the Patriots just a game away from a perfect regular season. In addition, Brady's season touchdown total stood at 48—just one behind Manning. And the Patriots needed just six points in the final game to break Minnesota's scoring record for a season.

But there was controversy. The Patriots had wrapped up the top seed in the playoffs. They had nothing to gain by winning their final game against the New York Giants (who also had secured a playoff spot and had little for which to play). Should Belichick risk injury to star players in a game that was little more than a post-season tune-up?

Belichick didn't hesitate. The Patriots had a chance to make history, and they wouldn't be satisfied with 15–1. Tom and the rest of the starters would play.

Surprisingly, the Giants made the same decision. The New York coaches weren't happy with the way their team had been playing, and trying to stop New England's perfect season seemed like a great test for their players. So in a game that meant nothing to the standings, both teams were going all out to win.

In a Week 10 victory over Buffalo, Tom threw his 183rd career touchdown pass. It set a team record, passing that of Steve Grogan, who had thrown 182 touchdowns in a New England uniform.

The Giants, led by quarterback Eli Manning (Peyton's younger brother), gave the Patriots all they could handle. In fact, the Giants led 28–16 in the second half. But Tom and the offense stormed back. They took the lead in style on a 65-yard touchdown bomb from Tom to Moss. It was a historic pass. Not only was it Tom's fiftieth touchdown pass of the season—breaking Peyton Manning's record—it was also Moss's twenty-third touchdown catch of the season, breaking a record held by Jerry Rice.

The game was a nail-biter, but the Patriots had done it—16–0! "What I'm most proud of is playing a playoff team on the road that was playing extremely hard," Tom said. "We found a way to come back and win. We did the same thing at Dallas. We did the same thing at Indy. We've been in some tough games. Everyone is going to enjoy this one."

The honors rained down on Tom after the season. He was named the NFL's MVP, receiving 49 of 50 first-place votes for the award. His final numbers for the season were spectacular: 4,806 yards passing, fifty passing touchdowns, and only eight interceptions. His 2007 performance was possibly the single greatest season any quarterback in NFL history had ever enjoyed.

❝[Tom] deserves it. I have thought for a long time that there is no past or present quarterback I'd rather coach than Tom Brady, and I am more certain of that every year he plays.❞

—BILL BELICHICK ON TOM'S MVP AWARD

"I am grateful to all of the voters for any consideration I was given," Tom told reporters. "[The MVP] is a tremendous honor and I am sure it is one that my family will one day look back on with great pride."

After a first-round bye, the Patriots cruised into the AFC Championship with a 31–20 victory over the Jacksonville Jaguars. Next up was the Chargers, who had pulled off a surprising victory over the Colts the previous week. The New England offense had led the way all season, but this time their defense stood tall. Tom and the offense struggled at times. Tom was especially having trouble throwing the ball in the strong, cold wind that blew across the field. But the Patriot defense held the Chargers without a touchdown. When Tom hit Welker with a touchdown pass late in the fourth quarter, the victory was sealed, 21–12. Counting the two playoff games, the Patriots were 18–0 on the season. They were one game—the Super Bowl—away from history.

Tom talked about what the team had achieved. "Being 18–0, I am incredibly proud of what we have accomplished thus far and I think we have talked as a team that for the rest of our lives we'll all remember this week, win or lose. We are all going to do our best to hopefully make that one of the weeks that we remember for all of the great reasons and not a week we would like to forget."

New England's opponent in the Super Bowl would be the surprising New York Giants—the team that had nearly ended the Patriots' perfect season in the last regular-season game. The Giants had made an unlikely run through the playoffs, winning three games on the road to advance to the Super Bowl. Just a few months before, the Giants had looked down and out. But Eli Manning had elevated his game, and the New York defense was stout.

Despite the Giants' recent success, the Patriots' run at perfection was all anyone wanted to talk about leading up to the Super Bowl. Was New England the greatest team in NFL history? Was Tom the greatest quarterback the league had ever seen? At times, people talked about the Super Bowl almost as if it were the Patriots' coronation rather than a football game. To many, the Giants were just the team that the Pats would beat to complete their historic season. The question wasn't whether New England would win, but by how much.

The Giants weren't ready to roll over and play dead, however. They took the opening kickoff and drove slowly and methodically down the field. The drive took almost ten minutes and resulted in a 32-yard field goal. The first quarter was nearly over by the time Tom and his offense finally got to take the field!

The Patriots used a strong running game and short passes to move the ball downfield. Early in the second quarter, Maroney capped the drive with a touchdown run to give the Pats a 7–3 lead. But from there, the defenses took over. Neither team scored again in the first half. The third quarter was also scoreless. The New York defense was frustrating Tom. A relentless pass rush was putting constant pressure on him, not allowing him the time to comfortably drop back and find receivers. To the shock of many watching, the Giants had managed to shut down the highest-scoring offense in league history.

The scoring finally picked up in the fourth quarter. Manning gave the Giants a 10–7 lead just a few seconds into the quarter. After the teams traded punts, less than eight minutes remained. Tom had always been considered a clutch player, and here was the chance to prove why. The Giants' pass rush wasn't giving Tom time to throw deep, so instead he worked the underneath routes. A series of short, pinpoint passes moved the ball down the field. Less than three minutes remained on the clock as Tom stood in the shotgun formation and took the snap. He saw Moss's defender stumble and quickly took advantage by throwing a dart to his favorite receiver. Touchdown! The Patriots were back in the lead, 14–10.

The Pats' defense had to stop the red-hot Manning. But the Giants' quarterback made play after play. They converted a fourth-and-1 play that could have sealed the game for New England. Then, on third-and-5 from their own 44-yard line, the Giants made one of the greatest, most improbable plays in Super Bowl history. Manning dropped back and scanned the field. Several New England pass rushers burst through the line, grabbing at the quarterback. Somehow, Manning slipped out of their grasp and heaved a desperation pass down the field. Receiver David Tyree somehow leaped, pinned the ball between his arm and his helmet, and held on as two Patriot defenders drove him to the ground. A few plays later, Manning finished off the drive with a touchdown pass to Plaxico Burress.

The score was 17–14 Giants, and only 35 seconds remained. Tom and the offense came onto the field to attempt a last-second comeback. Tom threw a couple of very deep passes toward Moss, but the two were unable to connect. Just like that, it was over. Shockingly, the perfect Patriots were no longer perfect. For the first time in his career, Tom found out what it's like to lose in a Super Bowl.

"We had a great season, we just didn't win the game," a dejected Tom said after the game. "Tonight doesn't take away from anything we have done over the course of the season. It's just unfortunate that tonight turned out the way it did."

A fourth Super Bowl could have been Tom's greatest moment in the NFL. Instead, it was one of his biggest disappointments. Who knew if he'd ever get another chance?

Epilogue

Tom's Legacy

Tom and the Patriots entered the 2008 season with every reason to be optimistic. They hadn't finished the job in 2007, and the 31-year-old wanted to make up for that. But unfortunately, Tom never got the chance to show his stuff. In the first quarter of the first game of the season, against Kansas City, Tom dropped back to pass. Kansas City's Bernard Pollard blitzed but was blocked to the ground. Tom calmly threw the ball down the field to Moss, who hauled it in for a 28-yard completion. But as Tom threw, Pollard lunged for his legs. Pollard's shoulder smashed into Tom's left knee, sending the quarterback to the ground, screaming in pain.

Backup Matt Cassel came in as Tom went to the locker room. Soon, Patriots fans heard the bad news. Tom's knee needed surgery, and he would miss the rest of the season.

Tom struggled through several surgeries, an infection, and plenty of rehab. Meanwhile, he cheered on Cassel and his teammates. The backup quarterback played well in Tom's absence, leading New England to an 11–5 record, though the team missed the playoffs.

Meanwhile, Tom had other things on his mind. On December 26, 2008, he asked Gisele to marry him. He did it while the two were in an airplane over the East Coast. The private jet was reportedly filled with roses. The couple was married on February 26, 2009, in a private ceremony in Santa Monica, California.

Professionally, rehabilitation on the injured knee filled Tom's time in late 2008 and early 2009. Some reports said that Tom's knee wasn't healing on schedule. Fans began to worry about whether he'd be ready for the 2009 season and whether his career might be in jeopardy. Tom, however, assured his fans that he'd be on the field come opening day of 2009.

Regardless of what happens in Tom's future, his legacy in the NFL is secure. No quarterback in league history ever achieved so much so quickly. He has excelled both as an individual and from the team standpoint. He has won four AFC championships and three Super Bowl titles. He's earned a league MVP honor and been selected to four Pro Bowls. His career record in playoff games is an amazing 14–3. Those are numbers that can stack up to any quarterback ever to play the game.

The list of all-time great NFL quarterbacks is short. Names like Montana, Dan Marino, and John Unitas lead the way. Tom

Brady's name belongs on that very short list. For much of his career, he was underrated and unappreciated. He had to fight for every minute on the field during his college days at Michigan. He was all but overlooked in the NFL draft. He was buried in the Patriots' depth chart until a teammate's injury gave him a chance to show his stuff.

Tom Brady is underrated and unappreciated no more. He is a future NFL Hall of Famer and possibly the greatest quarterback of his generation. He is living proof that with hard work and determination, even an underdog can achieve greatness.

PERSONAL STATISTICS

Name:

Thomas Edward Patrick Brady

Born:

August 3, 1977, San Mateo, California

College:

University of Michigan

Drafted:

Round 6 (199th overall) of the 2000 draft

Height:

6'4"

Weight:

225 lbs.

Throws:

Right-handed

CAREER STATISTICS

Year	Team	Games	Comp	Att	Yards	TD	Int
2000	NE	1	1	3	6	0	0
2001	NE	15	264	413	2,843	18	12
2002	NE	16	373	601	3,764	28	14
2003	NE	16	317	527	3,620	23	12
2004	NE	16	288	474	3,692	28	14
2005	NE	16	334	530	4,110	26	14
2006	NE	16	319	516	3,529	24	12
2007	NE	16	398	578	4,806	50	8
2008	NE	1	7	11	76	0	0
CAREER		113	2,301	3,653	26,446	197	86

Key: **Comp**: completions; **Att**: attempts; **TD**: touchdowns; **Int**: interceptions

GLOSSARY

audible: a change of the play called by the quarterback at the line of scrimmage

blitz: a defensive play in which defenders who don't usually rush the quarterback do so

concussion: a bruise to the brain

draft: a system for selecting new players for professional sports teams

dynasty: in sports, a period in which one team dominates a league, winning multiple championships

Hail Mary: a long, last-second, desperation pass

pocket: the protected area behind a team's offensive line, in which the quarterback usually operates

redshirt: a designation for a college player who can practice with his or her team but cannot play in games and doesn't lose a year of college eligibility

rookie: a first-year player

scramble: for a quarterback to run, either to gain yardage or to buy time to throw a pass

steroid: a type of drug sometimes used to gain muscle mass and strength. The NFL bans the use of steroids.

SOURCES

3   Don Banks, "Pats Take Thrilling Ride to Title in Huge Super Bowl Upset," CNNSI.com, February 4, 2002, http://sportsillustrated.cnn.com/inside _game/don_banks/news/2002/02/ 03/banks_insider (March 30, 2009).

3   Ibid.

4   Associated Press, "New England Shocks St. Louis to Win Super Bowl XXXVI," CNNSI.com, February 3, 2002, http://sportsillustrated.cnn .com/football/2002/playoffs/news/ 2002/02/03/rams_patriots_ap (March 30, 2009).

5   Charles P. Pierce, *Moving the Chains: Tom Brady and the Pursuit of Everything* (New York: Farrar, Straus and Giroux, 2006), 34.

6   Alex Tresniowski, "Super Cool Super Hero," People.com, February 18, 2002, http://www.people.com/ people/archive/article/0,,20136442,00 .html (March 30, 2009).

7   Pierce, *Moving the Chains*, 41.

8   Janice Page, ed., *Greatness: The Rise of Tom Brady* (Chicago: Triumph Books, 2005), 15.

9   Ibid.

9   Ibid., 19.

10 Ibid., 18.

10 Pierce, *Moving the Chains*, 45.

12 Ibid., 60.

14 Mike Sando, "Brady Puts Michigan Years in Perspective," ESPN.com, January 31, 2008, http://myespn .go.com/blogs/hashmarks/0-5-240/ Brady-puts-Michigan-years-in -perspective.html (March 30, 2009).

15–16 Mark Snyder, "Brady to Start in Spring Practice," *Michigan Daily*, March 20, 1998, http://www.pub .umich.edu/daily/1998/mar/03-20 -98/sports/sports4.html (March 30, 2009).

17 CNN/SI, "NCAA Football Recap (Michigan-Notre Dame)," *SI.com*, September 5, 1988, http://images.si .com/football/college/scoreboards/ 1998/09/05/recap.notre_dame. michigan.html (March 30, 2009).

18 Sharat Raju, "'M' Defeats State, 29–17," *Michigan Daily*, September 28, 1998, http://www.pub.umich .edu/daily/1998/sep/09-28-98/ sports/sports1.html (March 30, 2009).

19 Ibid.

19 Jim Rose, "The Main Event," *Michigan Daily*, November 20, 1998, http:// www.pub.umich.edu/daily/1998/ nov/11-20-98/sports/sports8.html (March 30, 2009).

20 Ibid.

21 "Squeezing Out a Victory," CNN/SI, January 9, 1999, http:// sportsillustrated.cnn.com/ football/college/1998/bowls/ citrus/news/1999/01/01/citrus _bowl (March 30, 2009).

22 Page, *Greatness*, 15.

24 Ivan Maisel, "The Brady Bunch," CNN/SI, September 7, 1999, http:// sportsillustrated.cnn.com/inside _game/magazine/football/college/ news/1999/09/07/cf0913 (March 30, 2009).

24 Associated Press, "Wolverines Hold Off Notre Dame 26–22," *ESPN.com*, September 4, 1999, http://assets. espn.go.com/ncf/1999/990904/ recap/nnxmmk.html (March 30, 2009).

25 Associated Press, "No. 4 Michigan Crushes Purdue," *CBS News*, October 2, 1999, http://www.cbsnews. com/stories/1999/10/02/archive/ main64681.shtml (March 30, 2009).

26 Associated Press, "Wolverines Can't Stop Spartan Combo," ESPN.com, October 9, 1999, http://assets.espn. go.com/ncf/1999/991009/recap/ mmkmml.html (March 30, 2009).

27 Associated Press, "Lions Lose Third Straight to Michigan," ESPN.com, November 13, 1999, http://assets. espn.go.com/ncf/1999/991113/ recap/mmkppb.html (March 30, 2009).

27 Ivan Maisel, "The Brady Bunch," CNN/SI, September 7, 1999, http:// sportsillustrated.cnn.com/inside _game/magazine/football/college/

news/1999/09/07/cf0913 (March 30, 2009).

30 Pierce, *Moving the Chains*, 90.
31 Ibid., 94.
31 Page, *Greatness*, 25.
32 Pierce, *Moving the Chains*, 126.
33 Page, *Greatness*, 30.
33 Pierce, *Moving the Chains*, 73.
35 Pierce, *Moving the Chains*, 129.
36 Page, *Greatness*, 36.
37 Boston Herald, *Tom Brady: MVP* (Champaign, Ill.: Sports Publishing, 2002), 28.
38 Ibid., 42
39 Pierce, *Moving the Chains*, 132.
40 Page, *Greatness*, 38.
41 Ibid.
43 Boston Herald, *Tom Brady: MVP*, 98.
43–44 Ibid.
44 Adam Vinatieri Post-Game Press Conference, Patriots.com, January 20, 2002, http://www.patriots.com/games/index.cfm?ac=gamereportd etail&pid=2096&pcid=41 (March 30, 2009).
45 Don Banks, "Move Over Paul Revere," CNN/SI, February 4, 2002, http://sportsillustrated.cnn.com/inside_game/don_banks/news/2002/02/03/banks_insider (March 30, 2009).
46 Page, *Greatness*, 72.
46 Pierce, *Moving the Chains*, 156.
47 Page, *Greatness*, 76.
49 Associated Press, "Favre Throws 300th Career TD Pass in Rout," ESPN.com, October 13, 2002, http://sports.espn.go.com/nfl/recap?gameId=221013017 (March 30, 2009).
50 Associated Press, "Given Enough Chances, Patriots Make Bears Pay," ESPN.com, November 10, 2002, http://sports.espn.go.com/nfl/recap?gameId=221110003 (March 30, 2009).
50 Pierce, *Moving the Chains*, 159.
51 Tom Brady Press Release, October 18, 2008, http://www.tombrady.com (March 30, 2009).
53 Associated Press, "New England 27, Miami 24 (OT)," Yahoo Sports, December 29, 2002, http://sports.yahoo.com/nfl/

recap?gid=20021229017 (March 30, 2009).

55–56 Mark Long, "Patriots 19, Dolphins 13, OT," *Yahoo Sports*, October 19, 2003, http://sports.yahoo.com/nfl/recap;_ylt=AnEHOIPyC0q6w _dindDu32_.uLYF?gid=20031019015 (March 30, 2009).
56 Pierce, *Moving the Chains*, 234.
57 Associated Press, "Brady Tosses Four First-Half TDs," *ESPN.com*, December 27, 2003, http://sports.espn.go.com/nfl/recap?gameId=231227017 (March 30, 2009).
57 Page, *Greatness*, 94.
59 Ibid., 106.
59 Ibid., 110.
61 Ibid., 119.
63 Ibid., 126.
63 Ibid., 126.
65–66 Jarrett Bell, "Steelers End Patriots' Winning Streak 34–20," *USA Today*, October 31, 2004, http://www.usatoday.com/sports/football/games/2004-10-31-steelers-patriots_x.htm (March 30, 2009).
67 Associated Press, "New England Curse: Manning Falls to 0–7 in Foxboro," *ESPN.com*, January 16, 2005, http://sports.espn.go.com/nfl/recap?gameId=250116017 (March 30, 2009).
68 Damon Hack, "Patriots Surge Back to the Super Bowl," the *New York Times*, January 24, 2005, http://www.nytimes.com/2005/01/24/sports/football/24afc.html (March 30, 2009).
69 Associated Press, "Patriots QB Limited Mistakes," ESPN.com, February 7, 2005, http://sports.espn.go.com/nfl/playoffs04/news/story?id=1985957 (March 30, 2009).
69 Associated Press, "Patriots QB Limited Mistakes," *ESPN.com*, February 7, 2005, http://sports.espn.go.com/nfl/playoffs04/news/story?id=1985957 (March 30, 2009).
70 Page, *Greatness*, 148.
70 Associated Press, "Patriots Hold Off Eagles to Win Super Bowl XXXIX," *ESPN.com*, February 6, 2005, http://sports.espn.go.com/nfl/

recap?gameId=250206021 (March 30, 2009).

71 Page, *Greatness*, 158.

72 Associated Press, "Johnson Runs for 119 Yards in Chiefs' Win over Patriots," *ESPN.com*, November 27, 2005, http://sports.espn.go.com/nfl/recap?gameId=251127012 (March 30, 2009).

74 Associated Press, "Patriots Throttle Jaguars as Champs Begin Title Defense," *ESPN.com*, January 7, 2006, http://sports.espn.go.com/nfl/recap?gameId=260107017 (March 30, 2009).

75 Associated Press, "Broncos Take Advantage of Turnovers, Eliminate Patriots," *ESPN.com*, January 14, 2006, http://sports.espn.go.com/nfl/recap?gameId=260114007 (March 30, 2009).

77 Associated Press, "Brady-Led Patriots Offense Outclasses Vikings in 31–7 MNF Win," *ESPN.com*, October 30, 2006, http://sports.espn.go.com/nfl/recap?gameId=261030016 (March 30, 2009).

80 Associated Press, "Crafty Brady Fuels Pats' Comeback Win over Chargers," *ESPN.com*, January 14, 2007, http://sports.espn.go.com/nfl/recap?gameId=270114024 (March 30, 2009).

80 Page, *Greatness*, 158.

81 "Patriots Lose Grip in Second Half, Fall 38–34," *Patriots.com*, January 22, 2007, http://www.patriots.com/news/index.cfm?ac=latestnewsdetail&pid=23856&pcid=41 (March 30, 2009).

83 "Star-Struck Moss Excited to Be a Patriot," *Patriots.com*, April 29, 2007, http://www.patriots.com/news/index.cfm?ac=latestnewsdetail&pid=25032&pcid=41 (March 30, 2009).

85 Associated Press, "Patriots Quash Doubts, Beat Chargers Convincingly," *ESPN.com*, September 16, 2007, http://sports.espn.go.com/nfl/recap?gameId=270916017 (March 30, 2009).

86 Associated Press, "Brady Lights Up

Cowboys for Career-High 5 TDs in the Duel," *ESPN.com*, October 14, 2007, http://sports.espn.go.com/nfl/recap?gameId=271014006 (March 30, 2009).

86 Associated Press, "Brady's Six TDs Give Him 27 TDs after Seven Games," *ESPN.com*, October 21, 2007, http://sports.espn.go.com/nfl/recap?gameId=271021015 (March 30, 2009).

87 Associated Press, "Manning's Late Fumble Seals Deal for Undefeated Patriots," *ESPN.com*, November 4, 2007, http://sports.espn.go.com/nfl/recap?gameId=271104011 (March 30, 2009).

88 Justin Einhorn, "New England at Indianapolis," *Yahoo Sports*, November 2, 2007, http://sports.yahoo.com/nfl/preview?gid=20071104011 (March 30, 2009).

90 Barry Wilner, "New England Patriots Finish Off Perfect 16–0 Regular Season by Beating New York Giants 38–35," *Yahoo Sports*, December 30, 2007, http://sports.yahoo.com/nfl/recap;_ylt=Ap38y6BRla6WqN_iXfyzrOT.uLYF?gid=20071229019 (March 30, 2009).

90 Associated Press, "Brady Takes 49 of 50 Votes in MVP Voting."

91 Associated Press, "Brady Takes 49 of 50 Votes in MVP Voting," *ESPN.com*, January 5, 2008, http://sports.espn.go.com/nfl/news/story?id=3182557 (March 30, 2009).

91 Santosh Venkataraman, "New York at New England," *Yahoo Sports*, January 30, 2008, http://sports.yahoo.com/nfl/preview?gid=20080203017 (March 30, 2009).

94 Dan Shaughnessy, "History Derailed," *Boston Globe*, February 4, 2008, http://www.boston.com/sports/football/patriots/articles/2008/02/04/history_derailed_1202113788 (March 30, 2009).

BIBLIOGRAPHY

Boston Herald. *Tom Brady: MVP*. Champaign, Ill.: Sports Publishing, 2002.

Page, Janice, ed. *Greatness: The Rise of Tom Brady*. Chicago: Triumph Books, 2005.

Pierce, Charles P. *Moving the Chains: Tom Brady and the Pursuit of Everything*. New York: Farrar, Straus and Giroux, 2006.

WEBSITES

NFL.com The Official Site of the National Football League
http://www.nfl.com
The NFL's official site includes scores, news, statistics, video features, and other information for football fans.

Patriots.com Official Web Site of the New England Patriots
http://www.patriots.com
Follow the New England Patriots at their official site, which features photos, videos, news, scores, and much more.

Tom Brady's Official Web Site
http://www.tombrady.com
Tom's site includes information on Tom both on and off the field, with photos, insider info, news, and more.

INDEX